Dalits and Dalit Representatives in Rural Local Governance

About the Author

Prof. Ganapathi Palanithurai, Rajiv Gandhi Chair for Panchayati Raj Studies, Gandhigram Rural Institute is an academic activist. His policy advocacy role at the Governmental level is increasingly felt at present in all the two levels, namely—regional and national as he does more fieldwork than theorization. He carried out several research studies in decentralization for both governments. His activities are supported financially by Population Foundation of India, the Ford Foundation, UNICEF, Rajiv Gandhi Foundation, Ministry of Rural Development, Ministry of Panchayati Raj, UNDP, SDC, World Bank, Action Aid, Department of Rural Development, Government of Tamil Nadu and DANIDA (Danish-Indo Development Agency) in specific areas of activities in connection with empowerment of people. He involves himself in capacity-building exercise for local body leaders. He has to his credit fifty two books, one hundred and seven articles in reputed referred research journals, twelve working papers, eighty two monographs, and thirteen review articles on three major areas, namely, Legislative Behaviour, Ethnicity and Panchayati Raj System. He has prepared twenty five commissioned reports for Government and multilateral agencies. He is associating himself with both print and electronic media to cover the issues of Local Governance. He was a recipient of Fellowship from Sastri Indo-Canadian Institute, New Delhi and World Academy of Art and Science, USA. He has visited the US and Canada, on academic assignments. He was a visiting fellow in the MiGill University, Canada in 1989. He held the position of Dean, Member Syndicate, and Member Finance Committee of Gandhigram Rural University. Currently, he is the Dean, Student Welfare, Gandhigram Rural University. He is a visiting professor in Cologne University, Germany. He is a member of the Advisory Committee of the Ministry of Panchayati Raj, Government of India. He is a member of Board of Studies of seven universities. He is a member in the high level committee constituted for devolution of powers to Local Bodies in Tamil Nadu.

Dalits and Dalit Representatives in Rural Local Governance

Voices from the Field

G. Palanithurai

CONCEPT PUBLISHING COMPANY PVT. LTD.
NEW DELHI-110059

ISBN-13: 978-81-8069-971-9

First Published 2013

Published and Printed by

Concept Since 1974

Concept Publishing Company Pvt. Ltd.
A/15-16, Commercial Block, Mohan Garden
New Delhi-110059 (India)
T: 25351460, 25351794, *F*: 091-11-25357109
E: publishing@conceptpub.com, W: www.conceptpub.com
Editorial Office: H-13, Bali Nagar, New Delhi-110 015, India.

Cataloging in Publication Data--Courtesy: D.K. Agencies (P) Ltd. <docinfo@dkagencies.com>

Palanithurai, G. (Ganapathy)
Dalits and dalit representatives in rural local governance : voices from the field / G. Palanithurai.
p. cm.
Includes bibliographical references (p.) and index.
ISBN 9788180699719

1. Dalits—Political activity—India—Tamil Nadu. 2. Representative government and representation—India—Tamil Nadu. 3. Panchayat—India—Tamil Nadu. 4. Local government—India—Tamil Nadu. 5. Dalits—Civil rights—India—Tamil Nadu. I. Title.

DDC 305.5688095482 23

To

Divine Mother

Preface

The 73rd Amendment to the Constitution of India is historic in many respects and of which reservation of seats for SC and ST proportionate to their population is foremost and significant as the hitherto excluded groups become included in governance and development. It creates expectation from the Dalit representatives of the rural local bodies that the issues of social justice would be administered very effectively as stakeholders. Further living conditions of the Dalits will be improved as Dalits representatives will take up the Dalit component plan in the planning process at the grass roots. Dalits representatives themselves expected that their status and respect in the society will be elevated. Academics and researchers have expected that the critical mass formation will lead to critical action by the Dalits leaders and thereby Dalits empowerment is almost certain but painful. Civil Society Organisations which work with Dalits began to feel that the Dalits representatives would take up all the untouched issues of the Dalits for redressal and it requires support from external agency. The above Civil Society organisations thought that they can extend support to the Dalits representatives when they face problem in the field.

Series of studies have been conducted nationally and regionally as to what extent this provision of reservation of seats to the Dalits in local bodies has helped for emancipation and empowerment of Dalits. Against this background studies have been conducted in EVR's land—Tamil Nadu to find out the status of Dalits and Dalits representatives. Conditions have not been improved as expected. It is obvious from the empirical studies that Dalits are in the design of the caste Hindus. The conditions of the Dalits and Dalit representatives give the impression that the Dalits have to face volley of problems and conflict at community level because of the presence of Dalits in local bodies as representatives. But there is one significant development we have noticed that Dalits have started their struggle. In this book, the first chapter covers the status of both Dalits representatives and Dalits in general. Second chapter gives the details of the problems faced by the Dalits representatives in Tamil Nadu rural local bodies. Third chapter is an account of the violation of Dalit land rights. It is based on the cases presented in a public hearing. It gives a sense that unless the Dalits are mobilised for transformation through a movement, the reservation of seats will not alter the status and position of the Dalits in rural Tamil Nadu.

Acknowledgements

'Evidence', a right based civil society organization, is functioning in Madurai and working with Dalits for their emancipation and empowerment. It is fully a support structure for the victims of the domination of the caste Hindus in the rural areas of Tamil Nadu. It conducts survey periodically on the critical issues of development of Dalits. They collect data, make analysis of the data and do policy advocacy. Beyond that the data have not been used for other purpose of writing research report for wider dissemination. Since, I am extending my support to the organisation at a small level, I have used all the data of the organisation. Whenever Rajiv Gandhi Chair for Panchayati Raj studies organises programme, Evidence is a key support organisation work with us for the whole programme. Evidence has provided needed data and for which I express my deep sense of gratitude to the executive Director of Evidence, Mr. Kadhir and his team. Secondly, I register my thanks to my colleagues in the Department and particularly Dr.V.Ragupathy for their generous support extended to me by allowing me to concentrate much on research and projects. Equally, my family members know that unit has been reduced to one, namely my wife since my daughter got married and my son got a job working elsewhere. Despite she is alone major portion of the day she never demanded my time and she patiently looks after me to perform my academic responsibilities without looking into my lapses in family responsibilities. Hence, I register my thanks to my wife Mala.

Finally, I have to thank the Concept Publishing Company Pvt. Ltd., New Delhi, as it unhesitatingly took manuscripts on local governance for publication. In my opinion, Concept is a leading publisher in India publishing books on local governance. All my works are field based and they are published in time before they lose their relevance and for which, I profusely register my thanks to the team of the Concept Publishing Company Pvt. Ltd.

Place: Gandhigram
Date: 17-07-2012

G. Palanithurai

Contents

List of Tables

List of Boxes

Introduction

This year Indian Government celebrates the 20th year of the 73rd Amendment to the Constitution of India as it is considered as historic and revolutionary. It is because the hitherto excluded and marginalized have been included constitutionally in the process of governance and development at grass roots. No doubt, India is a land of paradoxes. At a community level both constitutional provisions and community practices are at conflict and community practices overtake constitutional provisions. In order to bring changes at the community, Dalits have been included large in number to form critical mass. Constitution has stipulated that reservation of seats has to be given proportionate to their population. By administering many of the provision of the Constitution, relating to the social justice critical mass has been formed in India. The critical mass has to perform critical function. The problem faced by the Dalit in the society and in the process of development is critical functionaries. The task which had not been fulfilled by the State and Central Government has been shifted to the local bodies and that task has to administer social justice. With the assumption that the rural local bodies might have taken steps and initiatives in this direction, questions have been raised as to what extent the new rural local bodies addressed the issue and to what extent the conditions of the Dalits have been improved because of the initiatives of the rural local bodies under the leadership of Dalit leaders. Studies have been conducted nationally and regionally to see the impact of reservation. While looking at the issues in the present context analysis has been made as to what extent the Dalit representatives who have been elected to rural local bodies have been empowered. What are all the barriers they have faced in this process and what are all the steps taken to overcome the same have also been analysed. Subsequently to what extent the elected Dalit representatives have taken initiatives and in this process what are the problems they have been facing have also been analysed in this small work. It is a field-based study carried out by an organisation called 'Evidence' in Madurai city. Primarily, the study is conducted not out of academic interest or for knowledge building, but it is conducted for policy advocacy. While visiting the rural areas for data collection, it is not a mere academic exercise but it is a conscious effort on the part of Evidence to help the affected Dalits as support structure.

In this monograph, there are three chapters excluding general introduction and conclusion. First chapter is an empirical study about the condition of the establishment of the New Panchayati Raj system. In this chapter, the condition of both Dalits and Dalit representatives have been analyzed based on the field data. Subsequently, after the local bodies election in 2011 to find out what important changes happened on this front is yet another study carried out by the same organsation, Evidence. This study has focused its attention on the conditions of the Dalit representatives on the issues of social justice in Panchayati management. Yet another section deals with the violation of lands rights of the Dalit by the dominant caste groups. It is being looked at from the perspective of decentralization of powers. Finally, a general conclusion has been formed. Action points have been generated for policy advocacy.

The whole issue of inclusion of the Dalits is to be looked from the perspective of the Dravidian movement which was initiated for the social reform. Social reform activities began during the independence movement in Tamil Nadu. The temple entry movement began in Madurai in 1939 which was supported by M.K. Gandhi. Continuously and untiringly E.V. Ramasamy Periyar worked for social reform. Further, for the past forty years Dravidian political parties are in power by affirming the principles and ideals of E.V. Ramasamy Periyar. Despite all the above in the backdrop what is happening in the villages is the moot question which is being probed.

I

Exclusion and Inclusion: An Opportunity Utilization Analysis

Introduction

The present study seeks to analyze the problems involved in the process of inclusion of certain human collectivities which had been excluded in the process of development and governance of the society over centuries, through the new opportunities created at the grass roots in India at present. Historically communities and societies are excluded in the process of mainstream development either on their own because of their inability to compete with others or by the design of the dominant segments of the society who established hegemonic control over others[1]. The excluded communities had been continuously struggling for equality and equity with others[2]. An array of steps had been taken by the State to equalize the opportunities through affirmative actions and yet communities are not able to come up[3].

At this point of time a new initiative was taken by the State to allow the market to unleash the skills and capacity of the people with the developed technology and science by using the surplus capital to produce goods and services in the name of globalization. This new initiative has further increased the gap between and among communities and societies because of the increasing utilization of the capital, advanced science and technology to the market by unleashing the unlimited human potentials available in the form of skill and capacity of certain segments of the society. In the process of increasing gap among the collectivities, communities and societies, the country has witnessed increased conflicts and violence due to the increased awareness of the masses about human deprivation and increased human aspiration to enjoy material benefits and to enjoy democratic rights. In the triangle interaction among the three forces namely—State, market and society, the state is under the tremendous pressure from the market and the society[4]. To achieve economic growth steadily and fastly market needs series of steps from the state, equally society needs volley of measures to achieve equity in sharing the benefits of the growth achieved by the market. The State did act for the demands of both[5]. The crucial question is how the State is enabling the society to use the benefits of growth by proving opportunities to the most marginalized sections. Yet another issue is how the newly created opportunities are utilized by the marginalized groups?

Over a period of time, it was argued that institutions and organizations which were created for governance and administration continuously excluded and subjugated by certain segments of the society in the process of governance and development as the instruments of governance and administration were under the control of the dominant communities and classes[6]. Subjugation and exclusion of communities are by design or default of the institutions of governance but to find out remedy to the above problem, steps are being taken by the State to liberate the oppressed from the clutches of the dominant groups and include the communities in the mainstream development and governance process. It is strongly believed that of all the institutional mechanisms for governance, the representative democracy has got highest potentials to address the problems of disparities and marginalization. Equally, it has got vitality to empower the marginalized and excluded. In the newly created representative democracy in the liberated societies through its governance process, many of the socio-economic problems had been handled and enabling conditions had also been created for economic growth and development of all sections of the society. Thus, social transformation took place because of the initiatives of representative democratic institutions.

But the above assumption was also contested that even in representative democracy several segments of the society are left out in the development process. It is to be noted that at the dawn of Independence, the exponents of representative democracy looked at India with many questions as India declared that it was going to establish representative democracy. Because there were no requisite basic factors in India responsible for smooth and successful functioning of representative democracy. There was no middle class and the literacy rate was only 30 per cent. Social diversities and economic inequalities have kept the societies with lot of social conflicts. Hence, they suspected the possibility of success of representative democracy in India. But the representative democracy has successfully created the middle class and through the middle class an assurance had been given to the poor and the marginalized that the government will provide needed help to them. Only by assurance the poor and the marginalized had been managed so far. Now they have realized who have gained in governance and development and as a result they work up and started agitating against the existing governance arrangement and process. As a result, the excluded and marginalized communities are in struggle to liberate themselves from subjugation and to enjoy democratic rights along with leading a decent and dignified human life. At present, the State is enabling the marginalized communities to claim their entitlements as rights and for which they are facilitated to participate in governance[7]. When State is enabling the marginalized communities how the marginalized communities are able to make use of the opportunities is a question to be answered.

Setting

Before proceeding to make an analysis of the process of inclusion of excluded it is necessary to understand the existing conditions of the Indian society. Primarily, it is feudal in character and hence, feudal behaviour is being noticed even in democratic institutions. It is a hierarchical society based on the caste system. Collectively social relationship is determined according to the social status[8]. Further, the society is deeply afflicted with patriarchy[9]. Still 70 per cent of the people live in the rural India which has got dual governance namely constitutional governance and community governance[10]. Of the total population 58 per cent of the people rely on agriculture for their livelihood. As long as people rely on traditional farming operation and live in the rural areas their life is totally under the influence of the traditional community systems, processes and procedures. The British through their governance and administration tried to establish social equality among the different social groups by enacting laws and tried to remove the age-old barriers and practices. Yet they had a firm belief that caste discrimination and differences in India will continue to play their role and hence they tried to mitigate the ill effects of the caste discriminatory practices in India.

Though it was perceived by the Indian National Congress and its leaders that the approach of the British Administration was to create divisions in Indian society and to weaken Indian unity, they strongly felt that the caste discriminatory practices had to be removed from Indian society by the strong initiatives of the State system after India got Independence. Equally it was felt that it would be dismantled by the efforts of the social reform movement. The Indian National Congress and its leaders had firm belief that social discriminatory practices based on the caste system can be eliminated through the modern State system by laws, decisions, policies, programmes and resource allocations. The question here is how a backward society will respond to forward political instrument namely the representative form of governance. It depends on how social and political leaders handle governance instruments by mobilizing the people and managing bureaucracy to implement the constitutional provisions and welfare schemes and programmes[11].

Even after five decades of governance experience in achieving development through democratic decision-making, the ground reality has reflected the poor performance of the governance and administrative institution in delivering distributive justice. Having seen the ineffectiveness of the institutions at the federal and regional level in delivering distributive justice to the marginalized communities, it was decided to create a vibrant governance unit at the grass roots to achieve development and social justice for the poor and the marginalized by amending the Constitution of India[12]. Thus, the 73rd and the 74th Amendments to the Constitution of India were enacted by incorporating a provision to reserve seats in governance for marginalized segments of the society including women. It was perceived as an effective opportunity for them to claim their entitlements as rights with dignity. The new initiatives have enabled the marginalized segments to participate in governance.

The assumption here is that by reserving seats for the marginalized sections in local governance, hitherto excluded will be included in governance and thereby the issues of the marginalized could be addressed effectively. But the process of inclusion is not so smooth and the task is not so easy. It has hurdles, barriers and bottlenecks. But here the question is how these barriers and hurdles are being tackled. The grass roots organizations and institutions are not free from aberrations. Communities at the grass roots are functioning with the mandate and regulations of the communities[13]. When Constitution provides opportunity to the marginalized who have been excluded in the process of development and governance over several centuries, it is operationalised through the instruments of the State. As long as the provisions of the Constitution are not contradicting the existing practices of the communities, constitutional provisions are allowed to be operationalised. When constitutional provisions contradict with community practices, provisions of the Constitution are not allowed to be operationalised. Since Independence because of the mobilization of the communities by the social reformers and the initiatives of the states, all the parochial communal practices had been reduced wherever people are sensitized and conscientised on the process of social transformation[14]. Wherever social mobilization for social transformation is high possibility for reduction of social discriminatory practices is also high and *vice versa*. By creating an instrument of governance at the grass roots, the governance leaders at the macro level want to achieve at micro level what could not have been achieved over a period of four decades through macro governance.

Theoretically, speaking from the arguments of John Stuart Mill that the representative democracy cannot deliver expected results in the societies which exhibit high social conflict. Moreover, it requires high maturity on the part of the society to handle this representative democracy as this instrument is highly sophisticated[15]. Many of the countries in the world after their liberation from the colonial yoke adopted representative democracy for governance but within a short span of time they slipped away from the representative form of government in real sense. In a multi-ethnic, multi-cultural and diverse society with extreme social conflicts achieving development and social justice through representative democracy is really a challenging task[16]. Six decades of governance experience in India demonstrated that India has achieved material prosperity through economic development but it failed miserably in achieving equity[17]. The existing social conflict and violence in Indian society is the result of frustration of the neglected social groups in gaining access to material advancement to lead a decent and dignified human life. Though differences of social groups are constitutionally recognized and the discriminative practices are being tackled through different ways. But in reality and practice, discriminations continue to haunt the Indian society based on the hierarchical caste system. The disparities among the social groups could have been addressed through the affirmative actions effectively. In reality, they are not tackled as expected despite several initiatives of the government.

Thus, over a period of time, the governance system enabled the groups which are capable of using the opportunities to get advantage in the process of governance and achieve development. The poor and marginalized were not in a position to use the affirmative policies and programme to get economic advantage. The reason for not utilizing the opportunities is their disability and its multiplicity. The disadvantaged and marginalized social groups need enabling condition and facilitation to make use of the opportunities created by the government through affirmative policies and programmes. In reality, there was no enabling and facilitative condition. As a result, many social segments were marginalized. The whole process of marginalization, exclusion and deprivization had been thoroughly evaluated by the late Prime Minister Rajiv Gandhi and he brought out a proposition that unless the marginalized and excluded are empowered and made to participate in governance to claim their entitlements as their rights, development of the marginalized is very bleak and hence he found out a powerful instrument to address the issues of the marginalized. It is called new local governance and otherwise called "decentralization of powers"[18]. Though, he conceptualized a new local governance mechanism which was quiet different from the old one, he failed miserably to incorporate it in the governance system. But his successor P.V. Narasimha Rao, as Prime Minister amended the Constitution and created the new local governance system. The objectives of the new local governance system are the real milestones. They are: (i) it has to achieve economic development; (ii) it has to deliver distributive justice along with social justice; (iii) the whole process of governance has to be done through the participation of all segments of the people and through evolving participatory development plan from below. By doing so the process of inclusion of hitherto excluded in governance and development will be completed and by which Indian democracy and development will be inclusive.

Further, it is to be noted here that the reservation of seats for the marginalized in local bodies is only hope and an enabling provision but its implication could be seen only in operationalization of the same provision in reality. To see the implication an empirical study was conducted in Tamil Nadu as to whether the distributive justice has been delivered through local governance created through the 73rd Amendment to the Constitution of India[19]. In this study an analysis is made as to how the excluded are allowed to participate in governance and development by using the provision of reservation of seats for the marginalized. This process is based on the transformative process of the communities. How communities are changing their attitude and behaviours towards the marginalized by enabling them to participate in the governance and development process at grass roots.

Methodology

A combination of methods had been adopted to collect data from the rural areas. Data have been collected from the Dalit segments of the Tamil society. They are both SC and ST. The respondents consist of men, women, youth, retired officials, officials who are in service and all are from the Dalit Communities. Direct face to face interview with interview schedule, focus group discussions, and case studies have been used to collect the needed data. Further, for all discussions and recording of events, affidavits were obtained from the respondents. A group of investigators was involved in this process of data collection. They were oriented and trained in all the methods of data collection. They were divided into groups to visit the field. The districts were selected for this study based on the intensity of events and incidence of discriminations and violence against Dalits appeared in the news- papers. It is not a mere data collection exercise alone. Based on the requirements of the respondents who are affected due to discriminatory practices perpetuated in the communities assistance was also extended to the affected Dalit families. Many cases have been filed only after the survey was conducted based on the requirements of the respondents. The needed assistance was provided by an agency—Evidence. This survey was conducted by the above organization for policy advocacy work to be done in Tamil Nadu. Affirmative statements have been obtained from the respondents by getting the signatures. Further, for this work, the surveys conducted by other organizations have also been used and more particularly the survey conducted by Tamil Nadu Untouchability Eradication Front (TNUEF). The TNUEF has conducted extensive survey in Tamil Nadu on the issues of Dalits. Periodically, these organizations convene conference and highlight their findings. Hence, this study used the survey findings of the above organization. Here, it is necessary to understand the background of the organization which has conducted the above survey. The whole survey was conducted during January and February, 2011.

Evidence

Evidence is a non-profit organization working for Dalits, rights in Madurai and it is headed by Mr. Kadhir as Executive Director. It works extensively on various issues of the Dalit community in Tamil Nadu and other provinces. It carries out series of studies with simple methodological nuances to highlight the plight of the Dalits in Tamil Nadu. It collaborates with academic and research institutions to strengthen the research base of the organization. Evidence does not stop with carrying out studies and it goes further to build a support structure for the suffering individuals, families and groups of Dalits. For effective policy advocacy, it extensively carries out studies. After conducting the studies, the reports are placed before the experts for review and the same will be examined through a validation workshop. Only after validation workshop, the reports are taken for policy advocacy. It further periodically sensitize the young students from the higher learning institutions on the issues of Dalits through its training programme. It also organizes programme for Dalit officials those who are working in different offices with different capacities. Periodically, it conducts public hearing and taking many of the issues to court for the legal remedies.

Background

In Tamil Nadu 107.12 lakh (19.18%) people belong to SC and 5.74 lakh (1.037%) belong to ST. 63.2 per cent are literate among the Dalits. Of the total population, 22.9 per cent are in the rural areas. While looking at the all-India map, Tamil Nadu has the sixth biggest concentration of Dalits. 11 per cent of the Dalits in Tamil Nadu own land. Of the land owning Dalits 45 per cent own uneconomical and unviable small plots which cannot fetch any profit. Only 1.5 per cent of the Dalits are having more than 10 acres of land. There is no serious attempt to provide lands to the Dalits by the government. Even the Panchami land has not been identified and distributed to the Dalits. It was estimated nearly 5 lakh acres of Panchami lands available in Tamil Nadu. Equally another 5 lakh acres of temple lands are available. But most of these lands are under illegal occupation.

It is estimated that there are 1600 castes in India, and 76 caste groups are in Tamil Nadu. Of the caste groups, the Dalits are in the lowest position in the social order. They have to respect all the caste groups in the social order. But they are the most humiliated social groups in the society[20]. It is interesting to note that even among the Dalits one will find three sub-divisions. Of the 19 per cent Dalits, 9 per cent constitute Paraiyar, 5 per cent Devendrakula Vellalar and 3 per cent constitute Arudhathiar. Another minor groups constitute 2.18 per cent. Yet another interesting point is that Dalits maintain the sub-divisions more rigorously than the entire social arrangements. The strict adherence to internal sub-divisions and political party formations on the basis of the sub-divisions among the Dalits are the factors responsible for other social groups to subjugate the Dalits much easier[21]. The divisions among the Dalits are yet another sad story which has deepened the crisis. The hierarchy what we find in the caste system has deeply entrenched into Dalits also. The hierarchy is also maintained among themselves. Their living conditions in their habitat, their livelihood, health conditions and behavioural patterns are negative to the emancipatory process of Dalits. Dalit struggle started in 1957 through the murder of Immanuvel at Mudukulathur village. Yet another struggle broke out in Thanjore district in 1967 and it was for economic advancement through the leftist mobilization. 47 Dalit workers were killed. Later, the caste clashes took place in 1980s in northern Tamil Nadu. The same type of clashes took place in southern Tamil Nadu in 1990s. There were sporadic events, which provoked Dalits to mobilize for redressal. Dalits could not advance their struggle and they have not achieved results to the level expected based on the strength of the population of Dalits in Tamil Nadu. Though their struggle is on, they could not achieve much as other backward castes.

After the enactment of 73rd Amendment to the Constitution of India, seats have been reserved to Dalits proportionate to their population at all levels and thereby opportunity was created for the Dalits empowerment. In all the three tiers of rural local bodies positions have been reserved for Dalits. Ward members of Gram Panchayat, Presidents of Gram Panchayats, Ward Members of Block Panchayat, Chairpersons of District Panchayats, Vice Presidents, Vice-chairperson positions at all levels and committee members and Chairperson positions, Dalits have a share proportionate to their population. It cannot be considered as token. Really critical mass has been formed at every level by this reservation. The question here is whether the critical mass has done critical function. Performing the distributive justice is the critical function. This critical mass formation has been perceived by the dominant caste groups as a threat to them. This has created yet another struggle for the Dalits. The oppressor castes designed a power shift in such a way that power should be retained with them indirectly and for which the economic functional relationship with the Dalits has been used to retain power with them. Thus they see to it that their nominee from the Dalit should come to power and they should act as per the direction of the caste Hindu groups. As per the new design Dalits are mere nominal leaders but power is being used only by the caste Hindus. Otherwise panchayats headed by Dalits are not allowed to function. In many places, Dalit leaders are only proxies. In many places, Dalit leaders who are opposing the interference of the caste Hindu leaders are in deep trouble. In Meelavalavu Panchayat, the Panchayat President was murdered. In four Panchayats in Madurai and Virudhunagar districts election to Gram Panchayat was not allowed to take place for about a decade. In such a way, Dalits have to struggle to use power[22].

For a long period, the Dalit political parties were sidelined without making much inroad into mainstream politics of Tamil Nadu. The two dominant ethnic political parties, the DMK and the AIADMK though they committed for Tamil Nationalism, have not aligned with the Dalit political parties with fear that they will lose the OBC votes by aligning with Dalit political parties. Till G.K. Moopanar under his Tamil Manila Congress aligned with the Dalit political parties, both the DMK and the AIADMK had not evinced any interest to move with Dalit political parties. Only after G.K. Moopanar brought them into mainstream politics, the DMK and the AIADMK started aligning with Dalit political parties to face the general election[23]. Even after moving into mainstream political system, there is no improvement in the living conditions of the people of the Dalit communities. Dalits are in active politics. Yet they are not consolidated. No policy changes towards the Dalits economic advancement[24]. Even after capturing power in the local bodies, what are the conditions of the Dalits? And how their conditions are changing towards better? are the points of investigation. How the Dalit leaders in local bodies are able to address the issues of the Dalit communities is also another point of inquiry. At a cursory glance based on the small write ups in the newspapers projected the grim picture about the Dalit leader's initiatives in this direction. They themselves are in deep trouble. In this context, it is necessary to evaluate the conditions of the Dalits in the rural areas. It is to be noted here the strength of the Dalits in the rural local bodies in Tamil Nadu.

Table 1: Strength of Dalits in Rural Local Bodies

Sl. No.	*Positions*	*No. of Dalits*	*Total No. of Positions*
1.	District Panchayat Chairpersons	7	29
2.	Block Panchayat Chairpersons	91	385
3.	Village Panchayat Presidents	3,299	12,618
4.	District Panchayat Ward Members	162	656
5.	Block Panchayat Councillors	1,598	6,570
6.	Village Panchayat Ward Members	25,613	97,458

Source: Computed from Tamil Nadu Government Website.

Opportunity Utilization Analysis

Opportunity Utilization Analysis is a devise by which one can evaluate to what extent the created opportunities for human betterment are being utilized. It is to be done through a process. The process has certain requisites. Here opportunities are created for the women and the Dalits in the local bodies to participate in governance and by which the felt needs and unfulfilled needs of those segments can be better expressed and tackled. While creating opportunities enabling provisions should also be created to make the marginalized to use the opportunities. In the same way, while the marginalized are in utilization of the opportunities, a protective and supportive environment has to be created to move forward in tackling the issues of marginalized communities and segments. Mere creation of opportunities to the marginalized one cannot presume that their conditions will be improved. Conducive conditions are more important to make use of the opportunities. To create a conducive environment state has to play an important role and equally civil societies have to play a key role. Apart from the above, the marginalized should have determination to break the barrier. Even if they are ready, they should have needed skill capacity role and capability to handle the institutions. It is necessary that the communities which act as barriers to the empowerment of the marginalized should be sensitized on the conditions of the marginalized. Awareness has to be created among the dominant communities about the plight of the marginalized. Unless all the enabling conditions are created mere enabling legislation to reserve seats for marginalized will be of no use. Because we have seen many vital provisions in the Constitution are inoperative. Thus, to study the impact of the opportunities created, one has to look at from the enabling conditions and support facilities created for utilizing the opportunities. In the backdrop of the above, the impact of reservation of seats for Dalits and Dalit women has to be analyzed.

Analysis and Discussion

Details of the social background of the respondents, districts and village covered for data collection, and the discriminatory practices prevailed in the study areas are given in the form of simple tables. Of the 29 districts, 13 districts have been covered in this study for data collection. The above districts have been selected as these districts have witnessed high incidence of discriminatory practices. Villages have been selected based on the intensity of discriminatory practices. All the sub-groups of Dalits have been covered in this study.

Table 2: Details of the Respondents and their Districts

Sl. No	*Districts Covered*	*No of Respondents*
1.	Madurai	22
2.	Dindigul	33
3.	Theni	30
4.	Tanjore	14
5.	Thiruvarur	25
6.	Nagapattinam	17
7.	Namakkal	23
8.	Coimbatore	24
9.	Ariyalur	24
10.	Perambalur	26
11.	Villupuram	20
12.	Cuddalore	21
13.	Kanchipuram	21
	Total	**300**

Source: Computed.

Table 3: Social Composition of the Respondents (Gender)

1.	Men	224
2.	Women	76
	Total	**300**

Source: Computed.

Table 4: Social Composition (sub-division)

Sl. No.	*By Caste Sub-divisions*	
1.	Paraiyar	205
2.	Pallar	19
3.	Arunthathiar	74

4.	Kuravar	1
5.	Puthirai vannan	1
	Total	**300**

Source: Computed.

Table 5: Villages covered in the Survey

Sl. No.	*Districts*	*No of Villages covered*
1.	Madurai	13
2.	Dindigul	24
3.	Virudhunagar	17
4.	Sivagangai	15
5.	Thanjavur	17
6.	Nagapattinam	16
7.	Salem	21
8.	Namakkal	20
9.	Cuddalore	17
10.	Villupuram	20
11.	Coimbatore	22
12.	Thirupur	11
	Total	**213**

Table 6: Discriminatory Practices

Sl. No	*Types of Discriminatory Practices*	*Prevailing Gram Panchayats*	*%*
1.	Two tumbler system practiced	104	49
2.	Denial of permission to enter into common temples	213	100
3.	Discrimination in PDS shops	70	33
4.	Discrimination in Graveyard	208	98
5.	Discrimination in "Commons" utilization (Halls)	111	52
6.	Discrimination in "Saloon"	142	67
7.	Discrimination in water tanks and ponds	145	68
8.	Discrimination in Health Institutions	33	15.9
9.	Discrimination in Educational Institutions	29	13.4
10.	Discrimination in using the public toilets	58	27.2
11.	Compelled to carry the Dead Animals	185	87
12.	Denial of permission to use costly dress and Jewels	54	25.3
13.	Compelled to burn and bury dead bodies and carry death messages to relatives	183	86
14.	Bonded Agri Labourers	114	54
15.	Inter-caste marriage was strictly prohibited	213	100

(Contd.)

Table 6 (*Contd.*)

16.	Community Panchayats deliver judgments to the Dalits when they involve in petty crimes	105	49
17.	Ill-treating the Dalit elders by the caste Hindu youth by using slang	196	92
18.	Atrocities against Dalit women	94	44.1
19.	Compelling them to remove sewage of the village	158	74.1
20.	Dumping the waste of the villages in the Dalit settlements	104	48.8
21.	Property cannot be purchased without the permission of the caste Panchayats	63	29.5
22.	Dalit children are discriminated in schools	133	62.4
23.	Dalit students are involved in cleaning activities in the school	38	17.8
24.	Dalit children are ill-treated by using slang	126	59
25.	Dalit students are not permitted in public functions in schools	103	48.3
26.	Panchayat leaders are ill-treated	45	21.1
27.	Dalit students are not permitted to play with caste Hindu students	13.3	62.4
28.	Animals of the Dalit family should not mingle with the Animals of the caste Hindus	33	15.9
29.	Caste Hindu students are not permitted to take food when it is prepared by Dalit cook	63	29.5
30.	Postman will not deliver letters to individual houses of Dalits	33	15.9
31.	Discriminatory practices in village Administrative office	62	29.5
32.	Walls have been constructed to prevent the Dalits to enter into caste Hindu areas	47	22
33.	Dalits have to stand and should not sit in the public transport in front of caste Hindu	73	34.2

Source: Computed.

It is to be noted that Tamil Nadu is known for its transformative and reformative politics. It is modernized, industrialized, and most urbanized State. For about forty years Tamil Nadu had been effectively under the political regime of the Dravidian political parties known for their legacy of social reform. Plethora of laws had been enacted, innovative policies have been chalked out and innumerable schemes had been introduced to put an end to discriminatory practices and yet the discriminatory practices have been practiced in the rural areas indicate the reality of the Tamil society and politics. Dravidian Movement tried to create Dravidian identity and Tamil identity by dissolving the caste identity. The forty five years experience has created Dalits outfits to address the issues of discriminations on their own as the Dravidian parties could not achieve as they expected. The present study revealed the shocking realities.

There are about thirty three types of discriminatory practices practiced in Tamil Nadu against the Dalits. But the intensity of discrimination varies from place to place and it varies from issue to issue. But the discriminatory practices have affected all the segments of the Dalit society. Entering into temples, discrimination practiced in Graveyard, discrimination in using the common community hall, discrimination in using the village commons, discrimination practiced in barber shops, compelled the Dalits to carry and dispose the dead animals, compelled to burn and bury dead bodies and carry the death messages, not allowing the inter-caste marriage especially with Dalit boys and girls, compelling the Dalits to sewage clearance in the villages, insulting words used by the caste Hindus against the Dalit, discriminatory practices perpetuated against the Dalit students in the villages are more intense in the villages where the study was conducted. Children are affected, women are humiliated and youth are wounded and elders are also disrespected. It is a story of humiliation. They have no self-dignity and self-respect. They are not leading a decent human life as their habitat is being dumped with the collected waste of the entire village. Equally, they are not leading a decent healthy human life and dignified human life. Every discriminatory practice has its own dimensions and intensity.

Of the 33 discriminatory practices, 13 are very intensive. When the discriminatory practices are analyzed historically, one will find disappearance of many of the age-old practices. But new forms of practices have been developed. Many of the discriminatory practices are attached with institutions. Some are connected with educational institutions, a few are connected with temples and likewise many are related to institutional practices. Each practice has many forms. The forms of practices vary from region to region. It realistically identifies the forms of practices one would find several hundred practices are in vogue in the Hindu society in India. Discriminatory practices in temples are in many forms. In the same way, these practices are found in public institutions and in schools. Totally, the Dalits are leading a life in sub-human living conditions. Since they have internalized the above conditions in their life, it is very difficult to create awareness among the Dalits about their conditions. Equally, the dominant communities are insensitive towards the plight of the Dalits in the rural areas. It is only the Dalit youths are sensitive on their conditions because of their educational background and hence they get into conflict with established institutions.

Constitutional Panchayats Vs. Community Panchayats

Apart from the discriminatory practices, domination of traditional Panchayats over the rural society makes the life of the Dalits more oppressive and difficult. The traditional Panchayats are functioning in different forms. It varies from place to place. In the survey conducted in 167 villages, there are three kinds of traditional Panchayats functioning. They are: Single Panchayat for all caste groups functioning in 94 villages. In 73 villages Panchayats are functioning for each caste. In 14 villages traditional Panchayats are functioning for Dalits and non-Dalits. These traditional Panchayat leaders are called in different titles. The titles are significant for the community. The traditional Panchayat leaders are highly respected persons. All the traditional Panchayat leaders are not belonging to affluent families. The traditional Panchayats deal with variety of social issues of the communities. Family disputes, financial disputes between families and individuals, caste disputes, violence against women, land disputes, individual disputes, and activity against village pride are the issues dealt with by the traditional Panchayats. While dealing with the issues, the traditional Panchayats resolve the same by passing judgments. They inflict different types of punishments. Imposing fines, asking the accused to tender apology before the Panchayat council, asking the accused to prostrate before the Panchayat Council, beating the accused and imposing fines are the different types of punishments imposed on the Dalits by the traditional Panchayat Councils.

Table 7: Traditional Panchayats and its Role in Social Control

Sl. No	*Selected Districts*	*Selected Villages*
1.	Dindigul	167
2.	Madurai	167

3.	Theni	167
4.	Virudhunagar	167
5.	Sivagangai	167

Source: Computed.

Table 8: Presence of Traditional Panchayats and its form

Sl. No	*Details*	*Presence in Panchayats*
1.	Presence of traditional Panchayat	167
2.	Single traditional Panchayat for all castes	94
3.	Caste-wise traditional Panchayats	73
4.	Traditional Panchayats for Dalits and Non-Dalits	14

Source: Computed.

Table 9: Title of the Traditional Panchayat leaders

Sl. No	*Titles*	*Presence in Panchayats*
1.	Nattanmai	73
2.	Panchayatar	16
3.	Periyavitukarar	07
4.	Ambalakkarar	18
5.	Ur Periathanam	39
6.	Thalaivar	56
7.	Pannaiyar	08
8.	Social Leader	30

Source: Computed.

Table 10: Issues dealt by Traditional Panchayats

Sl. No	*Issues*	*No. of Panchayats*
1.	Family disputes	154
2.	Financial disputes	91
3.	Caste disputes	73
4.	Violence against women	103
5.	Land disputes	118
6.	Violation of community control	66
7.	Individual disputes	122
8.	Activity against village pride	66

Source: Computed.

Table 11: Types of Punishments

Sl. No	*Punishments*	*Village*
1.	Fine	148
2.	Tendering Apology	127
3.	Ostricides	50
4.	Beating	29
5.	Prostrating before the Village Assembly	45

Source: Computed.

We have a Constitution. We have a federal government. We have a State Government. People are governed by the laws of the land. Yet we have organizations and institutions are at the grass roots with strong roots in the tradition. It is always a conflict between the community practices and constitutional practices. Governance as per the laws are above the communities. All the community practices and subjugation had been highlighted in the media widely and yet remedial measures are not in tune with expectation. At the community level Gram Panchayats are created constitutionally for governance and development and more specifically for administering social justice. But the institutions are not allowed to take up the issue as they entertain fear over eruption of communal clash. Panchayats have tremendous potentials to tackle such social justice issues but the institutions are weak and unaware of the roles and responsibilities. One important aspect is that one has to consider in terms of opportunities to Dalits namely, the Gram Sabha a place for deliberative democracy. But it is not used by the Dalits effectively. Gram Sabha uses much information provided by many institutions and media to claim their entitlements. In such a way the space provided for deliberation has been used[25].

All case details are available with Evidence. Cases have been registered in the Police Stations by the active intervention of the Evidence for the victims of the traditional Panchayats. The details are given in table 12:

Table 12: Cases registered against the Traditional Panchayats

Sl. No	*Issue*	*Case Details*
1.	Devi (a Dalit Women) committed suicide because of the punishment given by the traditional Panchayat for her love marriage in Thittacherry.	In Thittacherri Police Station case has been registered against traditional Panchayat No. 120/2010-IPC 309.
2.	Traditional Panchayat inflicted a fine of Rs. 2000 to Mr. Thirumal for his remarks against the caste Hindu boys who were involved in raping his daughter. This incidence happened in Kodaikkanal, Dindigul District.	Case has been registered in Police Station with the help of Evidence against the traditional Panchayats. Case No. 167/2008 IPC-366 (A), 376 and 3 (2) (5) 1989.
3.	Mr. Nagaraj and Gurusamy had been attacked by the youth group because both of them opposed the decision of the traditional Panchayat in Valaynenthal Village in Ramnad District.	Case has been registered against the traditional Panchayat in Emaneswaran Police Station No. 54/2009.
4.	Mr. Thandapani of Mettupalayam village was beaten to death because he took food along with caste Hindus in Temple feast.	Case has been registered against the caste Hindus in Singanallur Police Station No. 261/2007-IPC 147, 148 and 302.
5.	Dalit youth were beaten for their participation in the village sports through their bulls. It was objected by the caste Hindus. As a result 8 Dalit youths received severe injuries in Peikaruppankootai village in Thanjavur District.	A case has been registered in Pappanadu Police Station. Case No. 22/2008-IPC 147, 148, 294 (B), 323, 324, 355, 307.
6.	Ms. Nagammal of Theni district was attacked by the caste Hindus for her involvement in demanding the entitlements of the Dalits in the ration shop.	Case has been registered in Kurangani Police Station in Theni District. No. 79/2008-IPC 451, 342, 354, 109, 506 (2), 376.

Source: Computed from the records of the Evidence.

Box-A: Traditional Panchayats in Maharashtra

A 42 year old Dalit widow Rekha Arun Chavan was tripped and beaten up in her own village (Malegaon) in Maharashtra, a most industrialized state, for the reason that her son Amol allegedly eloped with a Maratha girl Anita Desai. This incident happened in his own village of the Maharashtra Chief

Minister Prithviraj Chavan. People who were involved in beating up the poor widow had admitted and they argued that the community has taken such a decision. It was taken in "Tanta Mukti Samiti" (a traditional committee to resolve caste disputes in every village in Maharashtra) and accordingly the Dalit widow was given a punishment. The poor widow asked a question "would they have tortured me the same way had I not been a Dalit?" The whole incident took place in front of many that too in the presence of other Dalit men and women. Nobody prevented and interfered when she was beaten up by the caste Hindus. It is to be noted here that in Maharashtra there is a practice under Mahatma Gandhi Tanta Mukti Gaon Yojana (Dispute free village scheme) and under which disputes are resolved locally by a committee. The head of the committee is also from the Desai family. Though police case has been registered, the fact remains that the Dalits are still tortured and it is being done through a committee system and for which Government scheme is helpful. In this regard it is to be concluded that the discriminatory practices are in the Indian villages with different levels of intensity.

[*The Hindu*, 14th January, 2012, p. 14]

Discrimination in Places of Worship

Dalits are also no doubt Hindus. But as Hindus they find discrimination in temples. In every village there are many temples which are maintained by the communities mostly caste Hindus or dominant castes. The issue of discriminatory practice was discussed even during the freedom struggle. In many places temple entry became major events during the freedom struggle. By law, the discriminatory practices were abolished even during the period of colonial administration. Hindu religious reform movements outrightly condemned the practices of untouchability and discriminatory practices in Hindu temple. Further Constitution also prohibits this kind of alterations in social relationship among social collectivities on the basis of caste. Subsequently, steps were taken to prevent this practice and yet it continues to take place in the society. The conditions are not the same as it was before. There are remarkable changes in the society. Incidences of untouchability and discriminatory practices have been reduced but it exists in many of the rural pockets. Discrimination in temples is source of eruption of social conflict and they are being studied and explained in this work. See Table 13

Table 13: Discrimination in Temples

Sl. No	Types of Discriminations	Presence in Panchayats
1.	No entry for Dalits into temples	69
2.	No entry into cellar	72
3.	No ritual rights	56
4.	Temple car will not visit the settlement of Dalits	59
5.	Dalits will not be given any temple honours	52
6.	Dalits will not be permitted to pull temple cars	33

Source: Computed.

There are five major types of discriminatory practices entertained in the Hindu temples against the Dalits. In 69 villages, the Dalits are not allowed to come nearer to the temples. In 72 villages, the Dalits are prohibited to go nearer to the wall where idols are worshiped. Ritual rights are denied to Dalits in 56 villages. During the festival time temple cars are taken to all the habitats of the communities but not to the habitats of the Dalit community. In 59 villages, it was reported that temple cars were not allowed to visit the habitat of the Dalit communities. People belonging to all caste groups are permitted to pull the temple cars but Dalits are not allowed to touch the rope of the temple cars. In 33 villages, it was reported absolutely Dalits are not permitted to touch the temple cars. In Hindu temples honours are accorded to all caste groups but it was denied to the Dalit families. In 55 villages, it was reported that honours are denied to Dalits in the community Hindu temples. In all the above villages, Gram Panchayats are functioning and yet they are not able to do anything in this regard.

Land Rights of the Dalits

The poor living conditions are always attributed to denial of land owning rights to Dalit families. Owning land is an indicator of the social status. Social status is denied to the Dalits because the Dalits do not have land. This was the reason behind the granting of lands to Dalits during the British Administration. But these lands were also taken away from the Dalits. In the rural areas owning land by the Dalit families is not an easy task. Even if they have lands, cultivating the same is much complicated. In this regard, a survey was conducted in thirteen districts and in all the thirteen districts three hundred respondents have been contacted and they were all Dalits. All the respondents were affected by the land rights violations. Of them 82 per cent are affected by the caste Hindus 1.7 per cent of them are affected by Christians, 7.5 per cent are affected by private sectors and 1.7 per cent are affected by churches and 6 per cent are affected by Government sector. Dalits lands had been grabbed by all using different tactics. Mostly Dalits are made as debtors and by which their lands are grabbed by the other social groups. The details of the individual cases are in the Box-A. It is to be noted here that in Tamil Nadu slowly land has been transferred to Backward Class to Dalits. A new landed genre is emerging from the Dalits in the recent past despite all the hurdles[26].

Table 14: Land owning details

Sl. No	*Details*	*No. of Respondents*	*%*
1.	Owning Land	99	34%
2.	Not owning Land	201	66%

Source: Computed.

Table 15: Details of Acres owned by Dalits

Sl. No.	*Extent of Land*	*No of Respondents*
1.	Above 10 acres	03
2.	6-10 acres	01
3.	1-5 acres	28
4.	51-99 cents	07
5.	Less than 10 cents	48

Source: Computed.

Table 16: Details of lands owned

Sl. No.	Types of Lands	No. of Respondents
1.	Housing Land	50
2.	Wet Land	13
3.	Dry Land	32
4.	Land provided by government	45
5.	Panchami Land	12
6.	Housing Plots	10
7.	Lands under special schemes	12

Source: Computed.

Table 17: Land Rights Study Areas

Sl. No.	Districts	No. of Respondents
1.	Madurai	22
2.	Dindigul	33
3.	Theni	30
4.	Tanjore	14
5.	Thiruvarur	25
6.	Nagapattinam	17
7.	Namakkal	23
8.	Coimbatore	24
9.	Ariyalur	24
10.	Perambalur	26
11.	Villupuram	20
12.	Cuddalore	21
13.	Kanchipuram	21
	Total	**300**

Source: Computed.

Table 18: Composition of Respondents

Sl. No.	Composition	No
1.	Men	224
2.	Women	76
3.	Paraiyar	205
4.	Arunthathiar	14
5.	Pallar	19
6.	Kuravar	01
7.	Puthivai Vannan	01

Source: Computed.

Dalit Women Affected by the Caste Hindu Men

There had been lot of women affected by the caste Hindu men and they were not reported as the livelihood of the Dalit women depends on the caste Hindus. Further, even the male members of their families are not taking up the cases for redressal. Only a few cases have been taken up by the media and some of the political parties. After the establishment of support organizations, creation of SC and ST Commissions, and Women Commission people started giving complaints to these institutions. Media too started helping the affected individuals. Ill-treatment was given not only to ordinary Dalit women but also to other segment of the Dalit women. After the enactment of the 73rd Amendment to the Constitution of India, Dalit women were elected to Local Bodies in India. The elected Dalit women leaders have also been facing such a problem in Tamil Nadu. There was a classic case from Jegatabi Gram Panchayat in Karur district. Mrs. P. Chinnammal while making her presentation in a workshop organized by Human Rights Forum for Dalit Liberation in Chennai she narrated how she was ill-treated at Panchayat level, community level and in government offices. It is not only the case of Mrs. P. Chinnammal. Many such cases had been reported in the Round Table Conference organized by the Human Rights Forum for Dalit Liberation. Evidence has involved itself in taking up the cases for legal redressal. Now women are coming up for making complaints and ready to face the challenges also.

Table 19: Details of Cases who have lost their lands

Sl. No.	*Name*	*Incident*	*Status*
1.	Saminathan (37) Devinayakkanpatti Village, Dindigul District	He has lost 7 acres of land for Rs. 300 loan.	Case is pending in the court.
2.	Kamalakannan	He has lost 3.40 acres of land for 8 measures of grains. The land was given by the Government.	Case is pending in Palani court.
3.	Chenkeni Melapanthal village Villupuram District	He has lost 4 acres of land. It was grabbed for liquor.	Submitting petitions to Government.

(*Contd.*)

Table 19 (*Contd.*)

4.	Arumugam (50) Chinnakarattupatti Village Dindigul District	Government has given 60 cents to him and of which 15 cents have been taken away by a caste Hindu.	Case is pending in Palani Court
5.	Baskaran Melaulur Village Tanjore District	His father leased out two acres of land to Dharmaraj (a caste Hindu) for Rs. 16000. The amount was given back by him and yet he could not get his land back. He was attacked by the caste Hindu since he filed a petition in the Police Station.	No FIR filed despite his complaint

Source: Computed.

Table 20: Details of Sex torture to Dalit Women by the Caste Hindu Women who were affected and submitted written petitions

Sl. No.	*Details*	*Age*	*Address*	*Case Details*
1.	Kaliammal	24	Moongil Pallam Kodaikkanal Dindigul District	Case registered by Evidence 28.05.2008
2.	Panchu	14	Moongil Pallam Kodaikkanal Dindigul District	Case registered by Evidence 28.05.2008
3.	Kaliammal	35	Ayyakkanpallam Vedaranyam Nagapattinam District	Case registered on 25.05.2008
4.	Anjalai	13	Chinnavada Cuddalore District	Case has been registered on 15.06.2008
5.	Mallika	22	Thirumangalam Madurai District	Case has been registered on10.10.2009
6.	Muniammal	48	Periakulam Theni District	Case has been registered on 15.04.2009

Source: Computed.

Analysis and Interpretation

From the data collected and compiled, it is inferred that nearly more than thirty types of discriminations are practiced against Dalits in Tamil Nadu. All discriminatory practices are not in same intensity in all the districts. Some of them are more intensive in all-over Tamil Nadu. The practices such as, two tumbler system in tea stalls, denial of permission to enter into community temples, discrimination in graveyard, discrimination in utilizing commons, discrimination in barber shop, discrimination in using common water bodies, compelling the Dalits to carry out menial jobs are prevalent in all the districts with much intensity. Compelled to burn and bury dead bodies, compelled to work as bonded agricultural labourers, not allowing the Dalits to marry the boys and girls from the caste Hindu families, domination of caste Hindu Panchayats over the constitutional Panchayats, ill-treating the Dalit elders by the caste Hindu youth, atrocities against Dalit women, compelling them to remove sewage of the village, dumping the wastes of the villages in the Dalit settlements, discrimination of Dalit children in the village schools, the intensive discriminatory practices perpetuated by the dominant communities against Dalits. Dalit students are not permitted to play with caste Hindu students, and a few other, practices are not in the same degree of intensity in the entire place where survey was conducted. Six decades of representative democratic governance has not solved the problems of the discriminatory practices in the rural areas.

There are constitutional provisions, affirmative actions, resource allocation, welfare schemes for the improvement of the marginalized. In India the problem lies not in enactment of laws and evolution of policies and programmes for the welfare of the marginalized but it lies only in implementing the enacted laws and evolved programmes. The conditions of the Dalit are improving but not to the extent of expectation. In order to speed up the process of delivery of distributive justice, local governance institutional mechanism had been created. Further, representation was also given to the marginalized (Dalit) in the local governance institutions proportionate to their population. This proportional representation to Dalits in local governance has created a critical mass. The critical mass has to perform the critical functions. The representatives of the Dalits in rural local governance should have perspective, commitment, understanding, vision and strategy to work on distributive justice. By their active intervention, many of the problems of social justice could be solved easily. But there is no enabling condition for the Dalits to handle power efficiently and effectively and as a result they could not take up the social justice issues. Wherever they are taken up by the local governance institutions, social conflict and tension broke out[28]. A few leaders are able to succeed in their attempts and others failed.

Essentially studies have been conducted as to what extent reservation to Dalits has empowered them. It is revealed through studies that reservation has failed to empower Dalit women Panchayat leaders[29]. Despite the publication of sporadic events erupted in many places due to discriminatory practices, government is not serious and only a few political parties and leaders are sensitive on these issues. In many places, the Dalits had adopted a strategy to draw the attention of the government by leaving their settlements *en masse* and migrate to nearest forest of hillock. They vacate the entire village[30]. The problems are not addressed sensitively[31]. The allocated resources for the development of the Dalits have not been spent properly[32]. Many of the occasions, they are being diverted. Nobody to bother about such negligence. Further, there is no monitoring mechanism to monitor to what extent the allocated resources have been spent and programmes meant to Dalits' welfare have been implemented. There is no enlightened leadership to mobilize Dalit population under one banner to advance their cause by exerting pressure on the State and Central Government. There is no proper support structure for the Dalit Panchayat leaders to take up the issues of the Dalits at the community level through Panchayat activities[33]. The discriminatory practices entertained by the sub-groups of the Dalits with themselves acted as barriers to move forward in removing untouchability[34]. Many technologies added or aided activities will remove the Dalits from the bondage of performing certain manual works in the society.

Box-B: Paradox

It is to be noted here that the Government of Tamil Nadu had made a declaration that the untouchability problem persists in 384 villages in Tamil Nadu. Annually, the Government of Tamil Nadu is allocating resources for awareness creation on this issue among the people. Annually, Rs. 50 lakh are allocated and yet the problem continues. Here another paradoxical issue is to be highlighted. Government of

Tamil Nadu made an announcement that the villages where there is no untouchability will be given Rs. 1 lakh as award money. In 2010, only 31 Gram Panchayats got the award and it means in the whole of Tamil Nadu only 31 Gram Panchayats are able to apply for this award. It gives a clear impression that in most of the places in one form or other untouchability continues. In Tamil Nadu on untouchability issue 1050 cases have been registered. Normal conviction rate is only 5% in Tamil Nadu.

Box-C: Performance of Dalit Panchayat Leaders

A large number of Gram Panchayat Leaders belonging to Dalit community performed their roles and responsibilities very well. Because they were all trained fully oriented and enabled them to excel in their performance. These successes are attributed towards the role of training institutions and the support service provided by the training and research institutions. Further, they were all talented leaders addressed the issues of the Dalits through a new framework of governance without antagonizing the dominant communities. Many have crossed all the barriers. In all these places where Panchayat leaders have excelled, the other communities are positive towards the activities of the Panchayats. The leaders' vision, commitment, skill, strategy and capacity are critical to their functioning. All the success stories have been recorded and documented for wider dissemination[35].

Box-D: Dalits prohibited from using public well

Kodikulam, a village located under the foothills of Yanamalai (elephant hill) near here is a gifted place. It boasts of an age-old public well that provides tasty water round the year. People from far and wide throng the place with cans and drums to fetch the water home. But the Dalits of the village cannot dare even to go nearer to the well.

The SCs (Scheduled Castes) cannot go beyond this point, "Says a 61 year old farmer, A. Akkniveeranan, pointing to a distance of about 150 meters away from the well. They (Dalits) can ask any of us to fetch the water for them and we will oblige. But they cannot do it on their own. This practice has been there for ages and it cannot be changed", he adds with no shilly-shallying.

The caste Hindus of the village, occupied predominantly by people belonging to Kallar and Moopanar community, do not hesitate to talk about the discrimination of Dalits even to journalists. The well has been associated with four small temples built close to it and religious sentiments were given as a reason to keep the Dalits away from it.

"They (Dalits) will not be spared. Honeybees will sting them if they try to go near the well", says Packiam, an aged widow. Concerning with her, 26-year old P.Suresh, a construction labourer, says: "The youngsters of our village will be in these temples all-round the clock. Some of us even sleep here in the nights to prevent anyone from defiling this holy place."

The well is surrounded by trees that are home to thousands of honeybees. Strangers must be careful while nearing the well as the night suffers a sting or two. The villagers have intentionally left the honey combs untouched as it serves their purpose of discriminating the Dalits, "the bees do not sting us and we will not allow anyone to clear the honeycombs", says C.K. Aurtha Paiyyar, a 19 year old youth.

A lawyer practicing in the Madras High Court Bench here and residing at Othakadai neighbours fetch water from that well for drinking purpose. They travel in two wheelers to the village, which could be accessed either through the Government Agricultural College or from the Madurai-Chennai four-lane, and bring the water filled in cans.

"Once when I had gone there, some children asked me if I could give them some water to drink. I asked them why they do not take it themselves. They said they were not supposed to go there. Then, I understood and felt very sad for the poor children. This atrocity is being practiced there for ages and nobody is able to raise their voice for the fear of earning the wrath of the dominant caste", he says seeking anonymity[36].

Box-E: "Kudiparayan"

There is a system of bonded labour called "Kudiparayan" in some of the villages in Pudukkottai Disrict. 'Kudiparayan' is an individual from a Dalit family who has to serve the family of a dominant community and by which all manual works have to be carried out by Kudi Parayan. The wage is not as per the Minimum Wage Act of Government of Tamil Nadu. It is lesser than that of the approved rate. Normally, Kudiparayan used to borrow money from the family where he is working. Hence, he cannot demand. During festivals some free doles will be given. The same Kudiparayan has to perform the assigned duties which cannot be carried out by any other caste. This practice is in vogue in Pudukkottai district. Apart from those villages; this practice is in vogue in Sooranviduthi, Vaanjanviduthi and Dakshinapuram. Duties such as digging pits, drum beating for death, removing dead animals are assigned to them. Dalits cannot refuse to do it and if they do so, they will be tortured through social boycott and as a result their livelihood will be affected[37].

Box-F: Caste differences are legitimized

In many places, graveyard for each and every village has been created in both rural and urban areas. It is noticed in the survey that this creation of separate graveyard in the districts of Madurai, Thanjavur and Pudukkottai. Kappalar a village in Madurai district is an example of having 14 cremation yards for its 14 castes. Apart from the above, there is a Samathuva Mayanam (common graveyard) in the same village at Kappalar. This can be used by all legally. But Dalits are not using it as they fear caste violence will erupt over this issue. There are Panchayats known for its achievements in resolving such a crises of graveyard for Dalits by providing such a kind of facility by issuing a government scheme—Annaithu Garamma Anna Marumalarchy Thittam. A separate graveyard for Dalits. The debate is on whether the act of Panchayat is correct legally. One argument is that the Panchayat has to perform the social justice function by resolving the dispute. Naturally, the Panchayat has to make all the other communities to accept the dead bodies of the Dalit to be buried in the common graveyard. Then only the untouchability will disappear. But in reality the caste discrimination is in the blood of everyone and it cannot be done away all of a sudden. It will take time and yet the problem has to be solved hence Panchayat leaders instead of making other communities to accept the common graveyard to be used by all including the Dalits, a separate graveyard is created for Dalits[38].

Box-G: Wall to divide people on Caste lines

In many places it was a practice to erect a stone or brick wall to segregate the Dalits from the caste Hindus in Tamil Nadu. It was brought to light and agitations have been launched. A 600 meters long wall separated Dalits from caste Hindus at Uthamapuram village in Madurai district. It was brought to light only by the Gram Panchayat president who happened to be a Dalit. It is because a mass movement. The left political parties took up the case and fought for it. The State Government acted promptly and removed the wall[39].

Box-H: Opportunities are being missed

It is sad to note that there are representatives from Dalit communities in Parliament and State Legislatures. Apart from the above, there are representatives from Dalit communities in Local Bodies. We have IAS officials from those communities. Yet they are not raising their voice against the neglect of State and Central Ministries in implementing special component plan for SC and ST. Despite letter from the Prime Minister's Office and Planning Commission the negligence of implementing the special component plan for SC/ST on the part of the Central Ministries has not been either raised by the Legislators from that community or by the sensitive media. In the same way NREGA (programme) implementation can be used effectively for the Dalit land reclamation. But in reality, it does not happen all-over the country barring a few places. It was not noticed and raised by our representatives of the people. Many of the schemes meant for Dalits have not been implemented properly and huge unspent amount are being diverted. This was also not noticed and raised by the representatives of the people. Even the Dalit representatives have not developed Dalit component plan in local bodies[40].

Conclusion

In the land of E.V. Ramasamy Periyar and Dravidian movement known for intensive social transformation movement it has been noticed that the untouchability and discriminatory practices are in vogue in the villages based on the survey. Intensity and nature of such discriminatory practices vary from place to place. There are forty four types of discriminatory practices prevailing in Tamil Nadu. All practices are not in the same intensity. Despite the presence of constitutional guarantee and legal provisions discriminations dominate in the social relationship in the rural areas. It is obvious from the existing conditions one can easily draw a conclusion that these are all because of the lack of political will on the part of the State Government and indifference of the officials and police personnels. Further, it is also attributed that the political parties' indifference was also responsible for the existing condition. Moreover, the absence of social leaders to mobilize them continuously for social transformation.

The newly created local bodies are vested with two important targets namely achieving economic development and social justice. The newly created Panchayats are given responsibility to bring social transformation but whether the local bodies are equipped to carry out task is the main question. To what extent the newly created local bodies are able to tackle the issues at the grass roots is a serious question. From this study analysis, it is found out that they are powerless. Even the Dalit Panchayat leaders are not able to take up these issues because of the community pressure from below. The Panchayat leaders have not been trained in such a way that the leaders have to struggle in tackling the discriminatory practices at the community level. The Dalit Panchayat leaders are not allowed to take up the issues of discrimination. Since there in so support structure effective to the Dalit Panchayat leaders, they are not in a position to take up the social justice issues. Hence, the pressure of discriminatory practices in the rural areas, even after the creation of local bodies with responsibilities of bringing social transformation.

Recommendation

The Dalit Gram Panchayat presidents should be trained separately by specialized agencies which are sensitive on the issues of exclusion. With multi-pronged disability they have to manage the Panchayats to deliver services. In a hierarchical society, people from the lowest strata have to struggle to claim their entitlements and particularly they have to wage a relentless war to claim their self-dignity. The Panchayat leaders from the Dalit community never had an experience in handling power and institution. Hence, they require basic skills to handle governance institution and to deeper democracy by involving all sections of the society. So these leaders have to perform multiple tasks. Even after fifteen years of introduction of local governance, there is no worthwhile training package to build the capacity of the Dalits leaders in local governance. Unless their activities are nuanced, they can not become rich in social information and social justice activities. What we see in all training programme is "dos and don't dos" in the name of training. There is no support structure for the Dalit leaders at the ground level. All the research and support institutions are functioning at National level and doing research on the problems faced by the Dalits. But they never create ground level support structure for the Dalit local body leaders who are facing plethora of problems at the community level. Even higher learning academic institutions are also not sensitive on the critical issues of the rural society. They do research on several issues but they are not taking up these issues of exclusion for research and policy advocacy. In order to solve the problems faced by the Dalit Panchayat leaders especially at Gram Panchayat level first they have to be trained thoroughly on governance issues, development issues and issues of distributive justice as they have to perform in all those areas at the ground level. This kind of specialized training should be given by a specialized training agency and not in routine training institutions set up by the respective State governments.

Secondly, the civil society organization more specifically non-profit organizations which are working on the Dalit question should become a support structure not only to do research on their problems and in extending a helping hand to the leaders who are on struggle at the ground. Evidence in Madurai is an explain working for the Dalit leaders. This kind of institutions can take initiative to federate the Dalit Panchayat leaders at the State level, district level and national level to address their issues on their own. The women Panchayat leaders have demonstrated the power of the collectives through their federations. Tamil Nadu once was the pioneer in this regard, this model can be emulated by the Dalit Panchayat leaders and for which the non-profit sector organizations have to take initiative. Periodically, the Dalit Panchayat leaders have to meet officially in the government office premises and invite officials to their meeting and discuss their problems with higher level officials for redressal. Women Panchayat leaders federation in Tamil Nadu got a government order in this regard. By doing so the officials will be sensitized.

Further, the officials who are working in the local bodies have to be trained for handling the new context and they should be sensitized on the special needs of the Dalit leaders for their effective and efficient performance. Academic institutions more particularly the higher learning institutions can take up the Dalit issues at the local body's level for research through their projects, and student research programmes for intensive and in-depth analysis. Their findings and recommendations have to be communicated to the decision-making bodies periodically. Simultaneously, they have to disseminate their findings through media. The academic institutions have evolved tools for Dalit Panchayat leaders for monitoring the functions of Government Departments working for empowerment of the marginalized. By doing so the schemes and programmes for the welfare of Dalits could be monitored effectively and by which the delivery could be effective and efficient. The monitoring tools and perspectives should be integrated in the training programme. Periodically reports have to be prepared based on the experience of the Dalit Panchayat leaders by the research and higher learning institutions for dissemination and policy advocacy. In this regard, the research reports have to be sent to not only the Ministry and Government department but also the political party's leaders for taking them for discussion in Legislature of the State.

II

Problems Faced by the Elected Dalit Representatives

Introduction

Reserving seats for Dalits in local governance has created volley of questions as to whether the expected outcome could be achieved without much difficulty as the elected Dalit leaders have to work in the community. MLAs and MPs from the Dalit community are in Legislative Assembly and Parliament and they are not facing much difficulty in the community as representatives of the people. If MLA or MP or Collector from the Dalit community comes to villages, people from all caste groups meet them, give respect and submit petitions. People from dominant castes never question them and disrespect them. People know that they are from the Dalit community. They never argue with them. They can visit temple and they can enter into sanctum sanctorum. They are permitted to go to any place in the village. But the elected representatives in local bodies more particularly the Gram Panchayat presidents from the Dalit community face an array of problems and difficulties in the village. Conditions are still worse for the elected Dalit women representatives. But the mandate of the 73rd Amendment to the Constitution of India is to work for economic development and social justice. Fifteen years have gone after the establishment of Panchayati Raj what is the condition of the Dalits and Dalit representatives, in the rural areas. Serious studies have been attempted over a period of time to study the impact of local bodies in the community. Questions have been raised as to what extent the conditions of women and Dalits have been changed due to the steps taken by the local bodies. One will find variation among the states as the State governments have taken steps at different levels to empower the Dalit leaders through training, providing needed information to them in time and creating support structure for their function. Kerala is a classic case where one cannot find intense caste discrimination and intimidation to Dalits. Wherever Dalits struggled to overcome the caste barriers for their empowerment and development, the Dalits have emerged. An empowered Dalit leader never submits petitions. He or she struggles and achieves whatever he or she wants in Panchayat. But the Dalit who are in position on behalf of somebody mostly for caste Hindu groups face all kinds of problems. Whenever and wherever the elites tend to lose power they will evolve a design in such way that they handle power indirectly. Dalits in local bodies are driven by various forces of which elites driven is one which plays a dominant factor in deciding the outcome of action of the Dalit Leaders. One will find extreme variation among the regions of India. Tamil Nadu is known for social reforms movements conducted by E.V. Ramasamy Periyar for a longer period to remove untouchability. Further, the political parties' decented from the Dravidian movement of E.V. Ramasamy Periyar have been in power alternatively for about four decades. Apart from the ethnic political parties in power, there are Dalit political outfits in Tamil Nadu politics. Hence, expectation is more from this State on social justice. But reality brings a different story. Against this background a study is designed to assess the condition of the Dalits representatives in the rural areas after the 2011 elections to local bodies in Tamil Nadu.

Background

In Tamil Nadu Panchayati Raj systems, 26 per cent of seats have been reserved for Dalits, 25 per cent of seats for SC and 1 per cent for ST have been allocated. Of the total 12,524 Gram Panchayats, 3,136 Gram Panchayats for SCs and 156 Gram Panchayats for STs have been reserved. Totally 3,292 Gram Panchayats are under the leadership of the Dalit Presidents. One-fourth positions are with Dalits. In the same way, of the 99,333 ward members, 25,360 ward members are from Dalit community. There are seven District Panchayat Presidents from the Dalit community. There are 91 Block

Panchayat chairpersons belonging to Dalit community.1,590 Block Panchayat ward members from Dalits are in power to-day. 162 District Panchayat ward members are from Dalits. To create a change at the grass root level, the number of Dalit Representatives the Dalits got in local bodies are enough. Normal range of number for a critical mass is only 10 to 20 per cent. But in Tamil Nadu 26 per cent Dalits have got positions as they are reserved in local bodies for Dalits. They can exhibit a remarkable performance in local bodies. The presence of E.V. Ramasamy Periyar's social reform movement popularly called Dravidian Movement and its outfits. Dravidian political parties, increased literacy rate, fast urbanization in Tamil Nadu might have contributed substantially for the empowerment of Dalits. Presence of 26 per cent representatives from the Dalit community in local bodies has created lot expectations from the Dalit representatives. In the previous study, we found no substantial change at the grass roots. It is found out that changes are only in paper and not in the rural society. To study the reality a survey was conducted by the 'Evidence', Madurai based organization. It is a revisit of the same subject.

Table 21: Positions of Rural Local Bodies in Tamil Nadu

Sl. No.	*Seats*	*Number*
1.	Village Panchayat President	12,524
2.	Village Panchayat Wards	99,333
3.	Block Panchayat Chairpersons	385
4.	Block Panchayat Wards	6,471
5.	District Panchayat Chairpersons	31
6.	District Panchayat Wards	655
	Total	**1,19,399**

Table 22: Reservation of Offices and Seats for Women (SC and ST in Rural Local Bodies 2011)

Sl. No.	*Category of Reservation*	*Total No. of Seats*	*Reserved for Women*	*Reserved for SC and SC Women*	*Reserved for ST and ST Women*
1.	District Panchayat Chairpersons	31	11 35%	7 24%	0 0%

(Contd.)

Table 22 (*Contd.*)

2.	Block Panchayat Chairpersons	385	140	36%	87	23%	4	1%
3.	Village Panchayat President	12,524	4,289	34%	3,136	25%	156	1%
4.	District Panchayat Wards	655	228	35%	154	24%	8	1%
5.	Block Panchayat Wards	6,471	2,286	35%	7,526	24%	64	1%
6.	Village Panchayat Wards Member	99,333	33,121	33%	25,360	26%	1,039	1%

Source: Computed.

Methodology

It is an empirical study administrating interview schedule. Twenty researchers formed in ten teams visited the selected panchayats for data collection. First, the districts have been finalized and selections of districts are based on the incidents of discrimination reported in the newspaper. The researchers have been fully trained in data collection. Interview schedule was prepared and finalized with the help of experts.

Details of the Dalit Gram Panchayat Presidents Interviewed

Totally 171 Gram Panchayat Dalit Presidents has been covered in this study from ten districts. The covered districts are selected based on the intensity of social conflict reported in the newspapers. The details of the districts and number of representatives contacted are shown in Table 23.

Table 23: Districts and Panchayats covered

Sl. No	*Districts*	*No. of Presidents Interviewed*
1.	Madurai	24
2.	Sivagangai	17
3.	Dindigul	21
4.	Theni	21
5.	Coimbatore	13
6.	Erode	08
7.	Villupuram	19
8.	Cuddalore	19
9.	Nagapattinam	10
10.	Thanjavur	19
	Total	**171**

Source: Computed.

Since the intensity of conflict even among the Dalits based on the sub-divisions, respondents are selected from each division. The details are given in Table 24.

Table 24: Sub-division among Dalits

Sl. No.	*Sub-Divisions*	*No.*	*Percentage*
1.	Parayar	95	55
2.	Pallar	41	24
3.	Arundhadiar	35	20
	Total	**171**	**100**

Source: Computed.

In order to identify intensity of problem faced by the Dalit women representatives they are also interviewed. The details are given in Table 25.

Table 25: Gender

Sl. No.	*Gender*	*No.*	*Percentage*
1.	Male	87	51
2.	Female	84	49
	Total	**171**	**100**

Source: Computed.

In order to understand their economic status, how they earn their livelihood is ascertained and they are presented in the Table 26.

Table 26: Occupation of the Respondents

Sl. No.	*Nature of Work*	*Nos.*	*Percentage*
1.	Agriculture Labourer	59	34
2.	Coolie	10	6
3.	Self-Employment	21	12
4.	Occasional Workers	81	48
	Total	**171**	**100**

Source: Computed.

The whole exercise of data collection was completed within fifteen days of the start of the exercise. Twenty scholars were involved in ten groups. Since it is relating to social justice issue the organisation took care in recording evidence. After getting reply in the interview schedule, the researchers have got signatures from the Dalit Panchayat presidents. All the 171 respondents have signed in the interview document. Thirty-one members have given affidavit to file cases in the court.

Analysis and Discussion

With great difficulty, the investigators got reply from the respondents. The moment investigators reached the spot to conduct interview with the Dalit representatives, caste Hindus started monitoring the whole exercise, with great difficulty the Dalit representatives were separated and got interaction with them. From the whole exercise what the team found in the study is that the elected Dalit representatives do not have grip over governance and administration of local bodies. It is to be noted that unless the elected representatives are oriented thoroughly, it is very difficult to manage the Panchayats. Governance in India is much complicated. Governance at grass roots is complicated still further. At the community level constitutional provisions and community practices are clashing with each other. Dalits never had an opportunity to be in governance at the grass roots. Hence, training, capacity building and orientations are necessary to equip the Dalit elected representatives. Against this background, the investigators asked about their training experience. 94 per cent of the respondents had no experience in training as the training institutions have not conducted or initiated for conducting training to rural local body leaders. Without having any experience they are in power. To run administration, they need administrative manual but it is not given to them. In Tamil Nadu, there is no administrative manual prepared by the Government for local body administration. In the absence of administrative manual, the local body leaders run administration. That is why officials dominate the local body system. 95 per cent of the respondents informed that they have not received any manual for administration. 5 per cent of them said that they got some reading material from the officials. But they are also general, philosophical and history of local bodies not of any material useful to administration. Panchayat leaders should know which are all the offices and officials closely connected with Panchayat administration. 96 per cent of the respondents responded that they are not aware. There are about thirty-seven departments working in the rural areas and they are in contact with rural masses. But the leaders are not aware which are all the departments working in the communities with what scheme. They neither contacted them nor the officials contacted them. As per the government order, the Village Administrative Officer has to provide Village Map to the Gram Panchayat presidents and inform them details of Commons of the villages. 98 per cent of the respondents replied that they have not received any such Map from the Village Administrative Officer. Normally for any position the caste Hindus prepare themselves and contest in the election. But when seats are reserved for Dalits, the elites make a design and for which they draw the Dalits. 61 per cent of the respondents said that they have contested in the election and won the same not on their own. The above answer gives a clear picture that they are brought to the position by somebody. Who is the somebody is the question. They were driven to the space by others. For election, whether it is local body or Assembly election one has to spend money. Only 21 per cent of the respondents said that they have not spent money 78 per cent said that they spent money for election. But they informed that the amount spent was not their own money. Why somebody spends money for them is the basic question. It is interpreted as the elite capture. All the respondents replied that they are discriminated because they belong to Dalit community. 54 per cent of the respondents said that vice-President is a hurdle for their functioning because they belong to caste Hindu group and hence they dictate terms to the Dalit presidents. Only 30 per cent of the respondents said that they face problem in Panchayat administration due to caste Hindu clerks who are in the same Panchayat. 55 per cent of the respondents observed that they are always disturbed by the caste Hindu ward members. 61 per cent of the Dalit Panchayat presidents replied that they are insulted not only in Panchayat but at the community level also. 82 per cent of the respondents admitted that they are unable to function independently. 69 per cent of the respondents said that they are not in a position to take up the social justice issues. 3 per cent of the respondents said that they are not permitted to hoist national flag on Independence Day. 96 per cent of the respondents said that people in the village are against taking up social justice issues for discussion either in Gram Sabha or in Panchayat council meetings. 88 per cent of the elected leaders of Panchayat responded that the officials are not co-operating with the Dalit leaders for their effective functioning. 84 per cent of the respondents said that all issues in the villages are decided based on caste. 60 per cent of them felt that it is being used to abuse the Dalits. 72 per cent of the respondents admitted that there is no equality in the village. Caste Hindus either in organized way or individually always obstruct the independent functioning of the Dalit Panchayat leaders. 82 per cent of them stated the above. 68 per cent of the respondents responded that the castes Hindus are not co-operating with the Panchayat administration to remove encroachment. 88 per cent of the respondents said that the caste Hindus never support the development activities of the Panchayats towards Dalits.

Management of institutions, organisations and governments is the sole responsibility of the leader who is in the helm of affairs. Leaders are always made through a process of preparation. So leadership matters much after Dalits are inducted into the governance units of local bodies and as a result expectation from the institutions on social justice has increased. While making an analysis of the general impact, changes are not that visible as expected. But there are changes. The changes are due to relentless struggle of the Dalit representatives. But in certain pockets of the society a remarkable change one could witness. So macro studies are conducted in India to study the status of Dalits in India after the implementation of the 73rd Amendment. Micro studies through case study method have been conducted to establish the factors that contribute for the development of the communities more specifically the Dalits. It is to be noted here that from the national study, it is inferred that more than 50 per cent at the villages surveyed are under discriminatory practices. Dalits are not allowed to enter into the temples. Equally, they are not allowed to have access to water supply. Dalits are not permitted to sit along with caste Hindus. These are the conclusions of the national study.

At a point of time we discuss about the status of Dalit leaders one has to remember that Dalit as individuals and groups integrated and linked with the mainstream governing institutions through local governance. So far they were away from governance. Now they are part of discussion and they are the subject of discussion and they are in the transformative process in varying stages. Many are in struggle. It is to be recognized that the transformation of any community is through a process of struggle. Since Dalits are in the bottom of the social hierarchy, their struggle will be a long drawn and intensified one. Many of the occasions, it may be considered that the new local bodies brought more of social conflict than of development of the poor. It is true that social reality is exposed when power centre is created at the community level.

Table 27: Responses of the Respondents Discriminations against Dalit Panchayat leaders

Sl. No	*Question*	*Yes*	*Percent-age*	*No.*	*Percent-age*
1.	Have you attended any training after assuming office?	11	6	160	94
2.	Have you received any instructional materials to manage Panchayat	8	5	163	95
3.	Are you aware of the basic officials of new Panchayati Raj System	6	3	165	96
4.	Are you provided with the map of Panchayat area by VAO as per G.O.	2	1	169	98
5.	Are you drawn towards Panchayat election on your own?	66	39	105	61
6.	Are you drawn towards Panchayat election by your family?	71	41	100	58
7.	Have you spent money for election	134	78	37	21
8.	Do you feel that you are discriminated because that you are a Dalit?	171	100	0	0
9.	Are you disturbed because of the caste Hindu Vice Presidents	93	54	78	45
10.	Are you disturbed because of the caste Hindu clerk	51	30	120	70
11.	Are you disturbed because of the caste Hindu ward members?	95	55	76	44
12.	Do you find any insult by the caste Hindus at the community level	104	61	67	39
13.	Do you feel that you are unable to function independently	141	82	30	17

(Contd.)

Table 27 (*Contd.*)

14. Are you not permitted to sit in the chair of the Panchayat office	6	3	165	96
15. Are you not permitted to hoist national flag in Panchayat office	7	4	164	95
16. Are you taking serious efforts to address social justice issues	53	31	118	69
17. Do you find opposition in Panchayat coming to take up social justice issues	165	96	6	3
18. Are the officials co-operating with you for the function of the Panchayats headed by you	150	88	21	12
19. Caste based approach to decide issues	145	84	26	16
20. Dalits are abused in caste name	104	60	67	40
21. No equality in the village	124	72	47	28
22. Obstructing the Panchayat work by the caste Hindus	141	82	30	18
23. Dalits are not allowed to enter into the office	4	2	167	98
24. Keeping the keys of the Panchayat office with Vice-President	5	2	166	98
25. Keeping the register books with Vice-President	25	14	146	86
26. Dalit Presidents are Forced to sign all the documents	22	13	149	87
27. Not permitted to preside in Gram Sabha meeting	10	6	161	94
28. Forms groupism joining as a team and boycotting you	52	30	119	70
29. Sexual based violation	8	5	163	95
30. Assault	4	2	167	98
31. Denial to participate in public functions	44	26	127	74
32. Giving false information to the Government officials	61	36	110	64
33. Refuse to co-operate is related to removal of encroachment	117	68	54	32
34. No support and neglect in the developmental work for the Dalits	150	88	21	12
35. Refuse to sign the cheques	65	38	106	62
36. Not permitted to sit on the president's chair	7	4	164	96
37. Not permitted to hoist the flag	6	3	165	97
38. Forced to do menial job	2	1	169	99

39.	Refuse to announce about panchayats scheme	47	27	124	73
40.	Prohibit to write the name of Dalit President in Panchayat name board	13	8	158	92

Sources: Computed.

Major Specific Events

The elected Dalit representatives in Gram Panchayat from some specific panchayats openly come out and give it to the press that they are affected because of Vice-Presidents or clerks belonging to the caste Hindu. When it becomes news in the media it becomes abusing in the community. Once the Dalit representatives make statements about discrimination of clear message is given that he or she is ready for long drawn struggle for Dalit empowerment. The details are given in Table 28.

Table 28: Details of incidents against Dalit presidents

Sl. No	*Incidents*	*Details of Panchayat*
1.	Denial of right to hoist national flag in Panchayat office	Senthanadu Gram Panchayat in Villupuram district
2.	Denial of right to sit in the chair of the Panchayat office	Puliyurnatham Gram Panchayat in Dindigul district, Senthanadu Gram Panchayat in Villupuram district
3.	Physical attack on the Dalit presidents	Appanuthu Gram Panchayat in Dindigul district
4.	Refusal to hand over official records	Kottani Patti Gram Panchayat in Madurai district
5.	Caste Hindu vice-presidents control over the documents	Kadaneri Gram Panchayat in Madurai district
6.	Panchayat expenditures are with vice-presiderts and clerks	Thukkachi Kumara Mangalam Gram Panchayat in Thanjavur district

Source: Computed.

At a community level, the Dalit leaders have to face physical assault by the caste Hindu. Four Panchayat presidents have given detailed statement and they shown in Table 29.

Table 29: Physical Assault

Sl. No.	Name of the President	Name of the Panchayat	District
1.	Ms. Muthulakshmi	Ilangiyenthal	Madurai
2.	Ms. Baby	Athikombai	Dindigul
3.	Mr. Shanmugasundaram	Puliyurnatham	Dindigul
4.	Mr. Chinnan	Vagarai	Dindigul

Source: Computed.

Box-I: Humiliation faced by the Dalit Women Panchayat Leaders

Valli Deivanai(42) president of Pasavapatti village Panchayat in Cheurimalai Block, Erode District accused that she faced discrimination continuously in the village because she is a Dalit. She was not allowed to sit in the Chair provided for Panchayat president. Subsequently beneficiary selection for all government schemes had been done dubiously and she had been forced to sign documents as dictated by the Vice-President and Vice-Presidents of district Panchayat. The list prepared by them was not proper. Even while finalising old age pension beneficiaries; ineligible persons were included in the list.

A Kalaimani Dalit women village Panchayat president of Karu Vadatheru Panchayat was allegedly denied to hoist the Flag on the Republic Day. She was not permitted by the Vice-president to hoist the tricolour. She lodged a complaint in the Police Station and submitted a petition to the District Collector.

Panchayat Update, Vol. XIX, No. 2, February, 2012

Box-J: Caste Hindu Discriminate Dalit in MGNREGS

Caste Hindu of Putharenthal village of Ramanatahpuram District refuses to work in the areas of Dalit settlements under the Mahatma Gandhi National Rural Employment Guarantee Scheme (MGNREGS). This village appeared in the newspaper a few years ago for a rift between Dalits and Caste Hindus. Putharenthal Gram Panchayat allocated the work in the lands adjacent to the Dalits settlement but the caste Hindu refused to work in those areas. The caste Hindus refused to procure essential commodities from the ration shops which are located in the Dalit settlement. Workers in the ration shop carry the commodities from the shop and sell the same to the caste Hindus in different places. The caste Hindus insisted that a new ration shop has to be constructed for them in their area. Caste Hindus do not allow the Dalits to enter into their residential areas. The discriminatory practice had been referred to National Human Rights Commission.

Dalits have given petition—*The New Indian Express*, 10th July, 2012

Box-K: Caste Row at Nagapalayam

Dalits in Nagapalayam town Panchayat in Erode district lodged a complaint to the District Collector that the dominant caste groups constructed a wall and preventing the Dalits to have access to the main road directly. The Dalit children have to take a circuitous route to reach the school. By giving a petition to the RDO, the Dalits got a solution as the RDO opened a pathway in the wall. The Dalits were satisfied. In order to create a tension a few dominate caste groups took the dead body and reached the cremation ground through the lane created for the Dalits. Though there is a straight route to cremation ground, the caste Hindus took the Dalits lane to carry the body. While carrying the body dominated caste people threatened the Dalit women by showing the lethal weapons. Hence, the Dalits lodged a complaint to the Collector. The RDO who resolved the crisis earlier ordered an enquiry and based on the report action will be taken

The New Indian Express, 10th July, 2012

Conclusion

Society is changing. Attitude and behaviour of the people are also changing fastly. The caste discrimination is in the blood and it is being exhibited covertly and overtly. People those who are opposing the Dalits are changing their attitude towards Dalits. The change of attitude towards the Dalits positively is attributed largely because of their mobility, sensitivity and awareness and so on. But still untouchability is practiced in the villages due to ignorance. Still people believe that their social practices are above the Constitution of India. Further, there is no well meaning governance mechanism at the grass roots till to-day. Even though the Constitution granted community has not accepted the constitutional sanction of equality to Dalits. Now a mandate has been given to the Panchayat administration to administer social justice. In order to administer social justice, Dalits have been included in the governing team. When Dalits are included in the governing team Dalit leaders started looking at issues from social justice perspective and there one finds conflict. The nature of conflict and intensity of conflict vary from place to place. Even in the high intensity conflict districts one would find change on certain aspects of conflict. The way in which things move in the districts indicate that the condition will improve fastly and drastically if the State Government, civil society, media and officials working in Panchayat work proactively with Panchayats to tackle the social justice issues. Dalit representatives who are managing the Panchayats are explicitly bringing out the discriminatory practices being practiced against them. From the observation of the Dalit Panchayat presidents one can imagine what will be the position of ordinary Dalits. Dalit Panchayat presidents who are elected under the provision of reservation are no way different from ordinary Dalits. They are brought to this space by some forces behind the community. Though they are designated as Panchayat presidents their skill, understanding, awareness, capacity, capability are very low as other ordinary Dalits. Neither the candidates who are elected as presidents under reservation for SC and ST nor the State Government or the civil society tried to build the capacity of the Dalit Panchayat leaders to manage the Panchayats as leaders. As their awareness, skill, capacity and capability are low, it is very difficult to manage the Panchayats. Our governance, administration are always complex. It is very difficult to understand it. In the same way local governance has also been created. Training and capacity-building are *sine qua non* for effective functioning of Panchayati Raj. But it is the neglected subject in Panchayati Raj management of the State Government. Even while giving ordinary training, the social justice subject is neglected in the training programmes of the training institutions. Further, administrative manual is a tool for Panchayati Raj administration. There is no manual for Panchayati Raj administration. In the absence of administrative manual what officials dictate is the order for the Panchayat leaders. While even to claim his or herself respect the Dalit leaders are in struggle and in this context how Dalit Panchayat leaders will enable the Dalits to claim their rights and self-respect.

Box-L: What they want now?

- They want a separate exclusive training to manage Panchayats and administer social justice.
- They want administrative manual to be followed in Panchayat administration.
- They need state officials to monitor the social justice administration of the Panchayats. One Additional Director for Rural Development has to be appointed for this purpose.
- Panchayats have to be allowed to prepare plan development and it should be made mandatory.
- Dalit component plan has to be prepared at the village level and for which State Government has to facilitate.
- Vice-presidents position has to be filled in the same way as the position under reservation.
- Wherever presidents' posts are reserved for Dalits, Vice-president should also be reserved for Dalits.
- Dalits Panchayat leaders' federation has to be facilitated and supported by the civil society organization.
- Press has to highlight the plight of the Panchayat leaders and suggest policy recommendation to the State Government.

III

Voices of Dalit Victims over Land Rights Violation: People's Tribunal for Legal Redressal

SECTION-I

Introduction

For the emancipation of Dalits, land and education are the primary and key factors and they fought for securing both. Through education they are getting all development opportunities. But the lands given by the Government to them are not with them. Securing and protecting this land became problematic. Because of the lands of the Dalits are always the target of the caste Hindus and other dominant groups. Hence, the lands of the Dalits are snatched away from them by evolving different designs. Dalits fell victim as their attitude, behaviour and the level of awareness have contributed substantially for their fall. They are being exploited. Dalit organisations have been struggling for restoring the lands of the Dalits. There are civil society organisations enabling the Dalits to secure lands through schemes. Since land becomes problematic issue, a study was initiated.

'Evidence', a Madurai based civil society organisation has conducted a study throughout Tamil Nadu on land rights of Dalits. More than three hundred victims have given documents to Evidence as how they have lost their lands. In the past one and half years nearly eighty cases have been registered against individuals who were involved in depriving the lands of the Dalits by dubious means. Experience shows that 95 per cent of the victims could not get justice as there are many loopholes in the PCR Act and poor filing of cases in the court. Evidence has intervened in many of cases when they were reported in the newspapers. It acts as a support agency for the victims. While visiting areas of victims, Evidence used to raise hope and it gives assurance that it will support them. In the whole process of interaction, Evidence creates awareness among the victims and they are empowered. Evidence gathers documents for filing cases. How to get justice and, what to do further are the questions before the activists who are working with Dalits for their rights. Hence, a public hearing was organsied in Madurai by the Evidence on 30th June, 2012. In the public hearing there were twenty nine cases have been heard. Cases have been presented before the Juries. The Juries are: P. Sivakami, a retired IAS Officer, C. Chellappan another retired IAS Officer, Fernad Fathima, belonging to Tamil Nadu Dalit Women Movement, P. Shanmugan State President, Tamil Nadu Tribal Organsation, Prof. G. Palanithurai from Gandhigram Rural Institute, Ramani Mathew, a Lawyer and, P.S. Vanarajan, Director Manithan. More than four hundred participants participated in the programmme. All the twenty nine cases have been heared by the members of the Jury Panel. Series of questions have been raised by the Juries. They were all explained by the Lawyers who filed cases for them. Synopsis of the cases is given in the following pages for perusal. Full documents are available with the organsation, Evidence.

Section II: Cases in Brief

1. Dalit Women Ms. Chellammal was brutally murdered by Dominant Caste when she attempted to retrieve her land in Narasinganallur Village in Thirunelveli Taluk and District

Name of the Affected	Chellammal (55) (deceased)
Religion/caste/sex	Hindu/Pallar/Female
Address	W/o. Sundaram Muppidathiamman Koil Street Narasinganallur Village Suthumalai Post Thirunelveli Taluk Thirunelveli District

Incident in Brief	Dalit women Chellammal was abused by using the caste name and she was brutally murdered when she objected for forcing her husband to drink and got the land illegally by the caste Hindu in Narasinganallur Village at Thirunelveli District.
Name of the accused/caste	1. Mr. Sivan Pandian (47)/Maravar 2. Mr. Rajagopal (19)/Maravar 3. Mr. Chidambaram (45)/Maravar
Struggles/Obstacles faced by the victim	• She had scarified her life to save her precious land. • She was the sole person who fought to retrieve her lost land which was leased by her husband without her knowledge to the dominant caste and in the end she has to perish her life to assert her rights to land. • This brutal murder was in response to her making a complaint about illegal encroachment by the caste Hindus. • Fatal end when she questioned the dominant caste for illegally got leased from her husband.
Case registered details	Suthamalli Police Station registered case in crime No. 118/2011 under sections 307, 506(II) I.P.C. r/w 3(1)(10), 3(2)(5)SC/ST Act @302 I.P.C.
Interventions	1. Fact-finding was done by the Evidence team on 15.04.2011. 2. On 18.04.2011 family members of the deceased victim approached Evidence office directly. 3. Brief counselling was done for the victim's family members. 4. Press release was given to media to highlight the news to public. 5. Complaints preferred to State Human Rights Commission, National SC/ST Commission, State Women Commission, Chief Secretary, DGP, ADW SC, District Collector, Thirunelveli, Superintendent of Police, Thirunelveli, DSP, Cheranmadevi on 19.04.2011.
Impact	• Suthamali police had registered FIR in Cr.No.118/11 under IPC section 307, 506(2) r/w 3(1) (10), 3(2) (5) SC/ST Act @302 IPC. • Accused was arrested immediately. • Victim's family members were encouraged and motivated to speak and take up the issue further on their own. • Authentic documents were gathered by the team to prosecute the perpetrators. • The victim's family members are now well aware of the laws for reclaiming the rights related to land. • Strategically we were able to expose in getting

	justice to the affected by sending various complaints to various Government agencies and Commissions. • PRC No. 31/2011 was pending in the Court of Judicial Magistrate, Cheranmadevi. • A sum of Rs. 1.50 lakhs was awarded to the legal heir of deceased victim.
List of documents	1. Copy of FIR in Cr.No.118/2011 dated 10.04.2011 2. Death certificate of deceased victim 3. Postmortem certificate 4. Press release dated 18.04.2011 5. Copy of complaint of Lakshmanan dated 18.04.2011 6. Response from National Commission for Scheduled Caste Chennai dated 26.04.2011

Source: Generated from Evidence, Voices of Dalit Victim—Land Rights Violation: People's Tribunal for Legal Redressal, Vol. I, Madurai: Evidence, 2012.

2. Dalit women Karuppammal was abused in caste name and intimidated to kill for seeking justice over occupying her 1.59 acres own land illegally by dominant caste in Thattankulam Village, Palani Taluk in Dindigul District

Name of the Affected	Karuppammal (43)
Religion/caste/sex	Hindu/Arunthathiar/Female
Address	W/o. Ramu. 122/1, North Street, Thattankulam Village Palani Taluk Dindigul District
Incident in Brief	Dalit woman Karuppammal (43) W/o. Ramu, a resident of Thattankulam Village, Palani Taluk at Dindigul District was abused in caste name and intimidated to kill her by caste Hindu Subbramani and his brother Arumugam while victim opposed for occupying her land illegally and forcibly by the caste Hindus.
Name of the accused/caste	1. Mr. Subramni (45)/Goundar 2 Mr. Arumugam (43)/Goundar
Struggles/Obstacles faced by the victim	• Affected Dalit woman has been continuously fighting but inability to own her land for the past 12 years • Police has received victim's complaint but refused to file case and take necessary action. • The caste Hindu Kandasami cheated and prepared forged document under sale deed and enjoyed land owned by the victim's grandfather Vellai Mathari whose signature was not found in sale deed.

	• After the death of caste Hindu Kandasamy, when the victim approached to retrieve the land, his sons objected and threatened to kill the victim.
Case registered details	Police complaint preferred by registered post in the Thali Police Station at Thirupur District dated 17.05.2011. FIR was filed by the police since the caste Hindus filed suit in civil court.
Interventions	1. Victim directly approached Evidence on 17.05.2011. 2. Supportive counselling was given to the affected victim. 3. Sensitized the woman victim to know more about the laws relating to land rights and preventing them getting exploited by the accused. 4. Complaints were sent to State Human Rights Commission, National SC/ST Commission, State Women Commission, Chief Secretary, DGP, Superintendent of Police, DSP, Inspector and RDO Udumalapettai on 17.05.2011. 5. RTI was sent to know the present status of the case on 28.07.2011 6. Case was filed before the High Court, Madurai bench to seek order to retrieve the land and file charge sheet against the accused and pending in the court
Impact	• Tamil Nadu State Women Commission and State Human Rights Commission forwarded to SP Dindigul to look into this matter. • Superintendent of Police, Dindigul had forwarded letter to SP, Coimbatore to take necessary action. • Authentic documents were gathered by the team to prosecute the perpetrators. • Due to the assistance of Evidence the Dalit woman is able to approach the Court to seek justice. • The victim is able to regain control over her emotions. • The victim is now well aware of the laws to reclaim their rights related to land. • Reply received under RTI Act from Superintendent of Police, Thirupur on 18.08.2011.
List of documents	1. Copy of the patta in the name of victim's mother Makaliammal. 2. Adangal account copy 3. Land tax receipts 4. Forged sale deed 5. Copy of complaint by Karuppammmal dated 17.05.2011 6. Response from Tamil Nadu State Commission for Women, Chennai dated 27.05.2011

Source: Computed from the Evidence document cited for case-I.

3. Dalit women Puspam (48) and other Dalits were abused in caste name and threatened to kill by the caste Hindu when objected the illegal encroachment of their land at Kondamari Village, Madurai North Taluk, Madurai District

Name of the Affected	Puspam (48)
Religion/Caste/Sex	Hindu/Parayar/Female
Address	8/45, Kindamari Village, Paravai Post. Madurai North Taluk Madurai District.
Incident in Brief	Dalit woman Puspam (48) w/o, Krishnan a resident of Vilankudi Village at Madurai District and some of her community people were abused in caste name and were threatened to be murdered by caste Christians when victim and other Dalits objected to the illegal encroachment of their lands by caste Hindus.
Name of the accused/Caste	1. Mr. Gnanaoli (60)/Christian caste Hindu 2. Mr. Jesuraj (49)/Christian caste Hindu 3. Mr. Jeyaraj (45)/Christian caste Hindu 4. Mr. Sahayaraj (43)/Christian caste Hindu 5. Mr. Seemanraj (40)/Christian caste Hindu
Struggles/Obstacles/Caste	• Though the victim and her community members were residing in their locality gifted by Thiruvavaduthurai Athinam religious endowment for more than 40 years, people are struggling to get legal ownership for their own land since 12 years. • Meantime an influenced caste Hindu encroached the land illegally and intimidating the people. • Dalit family members and community members have lost their daily earnings as they were asked to meet the officials often and justice is delayed for the affected. • As the value of the disputed land has gone high the risks also gone high. It is a challenge to the local people to restore back their land.

Case registered details	Koodalputhur police had registered FIR in Cr.No.138/2010 under IPC section 294(b), 323, 506(1) on 05.04.2010.
Interventions	1. On 5.01.2012 victim directly reported to Evidence office. 2. Supportive counselling was given to the affected victim and her family members. 3. Educated the Dalit victim to understand the laws relating to land rights violations and stop getting exploited by their opponents. 4. Complaints preferred to State Human Rights Commission, National SC/ST Commission, State Women Commission, Chief Secretary, DGP, ADW SC, District Collector Madurai, SP Madurai, DSP Samayanallur, Inspector of Police, Koodalputhur on 9.01.2012.
Impact	• Koodalputhur police had registered FIR in Cr.No.138/2010 under section 294(b), 323,506(1) IPC. • Strategically we were able to expose in getting justice to the affected by sending various complaints to various Government agencies and Commissions. • Authentic documents were collected by the team to prosecute the perpetrators. • Due to our assistance the Dalit woman was able to approach the legal system to seek redress. • The Dalit woman victim is now well aware of the laws to reclaim their rights. • Response from Tamil Nadu State Commission for Women, Chennai dated 22.03.2012. • Reply received under RTI Act on 13.04.2012. • Letter addressed to Thiruvavaduthurai Athinam, Nagai by Tahsildar, Madurai north dated 14.05.2012.
List of documents	1. Copy of order District Munsif, Madurai Taluk Madurai in O.S.No. 248/2006 dated 17.12.2009. 2. Copy of FIR in Cr.No.138/2010 dated 5.4.2010. 3. Copy of layout for S.No. 62/1

Source: Evidence Document.

4. Dalit woman Rani and community members were abused in caste name and assaulted with deadly weapons by the caste Hindu Panchayat president during land measurement allotted to Dalits in Vidathakulam Village in Madurai District

Name of the Affected	Rani (38)
Religion/caste/sex	Hindu/Pallan/Female
Address	W/o. Chandiran, South Street, Anandan Nagar, Vidathakulam Village, Vidathakulam Post, Thirumangalam Taluk, Madurai District.
Incident in Brief	Dalit woman Rani (38) W/o Chandiran resident of Vidathakulam Village, Thirumangalam Taluk at Madurai district and her community people were abused in caste name and brutally assaulted by caste Hindu Panchayat president Ramamoorthy and his gang over a land dispute. The caste Hindus also prevented the government officials from measuring the land allotted to Dalit.
Name of the accused/caste	1. Mr. Ramamoorthy (45)/Naicker 2. Mr. Shiva 3. Mr. Sooryanarayanan 4. Mr. Jeyaraman 5. Mr. Anandaraj 6. Mr. Ayyadurai
Sruggles/Obstacles faced by the victim	• Though victim and community members were given patta land in 2010 by the government, land was not measured; they were not allowed to live in peace. • Further, the victim and community members fought against the false case filed by the caste Hindus. • Dalit women are not aware of their land rights since 2010 and were facing constant threat and lived under fear from caste Hindu Panchayat president. • Counter-complaint was filed against Dalits following the complaint preferred by Dalit over land dispute.
Caste registered details	Thirumangalam Taluk police had registered FIR in Cr.No.168/11 under IPC section 147,148,323,324,427 r/w 3(1)(10) SC/ST Act on 25.06.2011.
Interventions	• Fact-finding was done by Evidence team on 27.06.2011.

	• Victim approached Evidence office directly on 28.06.2011. • Educated woman victim to understand the laws relating to land rights violations and stop getting exploited by their opponents. • Supportive counselling was given to the affected victim and her family members. • Complaints preferred to State Human Rights Commission, National SC/ST Commission, State Women Commission, Chief Secretary, DGP, ADW SC, District Collector Madurai, SP Madurai, and DSP Thirumangalam on 29.06.2011. • Case was filed before High Court Madurai bench seeking for filing charge sheet and inclusion of Section 3(1)(4) of SC/ST Act on 11.07.2011 • The victim sent the letter to the National Commission for Scheduled Caste, Chennai to give report if received from Superintendent of Police, Madurai district.
Impact	• Thirumangalam Taluk police had registered FIR in Cr.No.168/11 under IPC section 147,148,323,324,427 r/w 3(1)(10) SC/ST Act on 25.06.2011. • National Commission for Scheduled Caste had forwarded letter to Superintendent of Police, Madurai to look into the matter on 18.07.2011. • Accused was arrested by the police. • Strategically we were able to expose in getting justice to the affected by sending various complaints to various Government Offices and Commissions. • Authentic documents were collected by the team to prosecute the perpetrators. • Due to our assistance the Dalit woman was able to approach the legal institutions to seek redressal. • The Dalit woman victim is now well aware of the laws to reclaim their rights related to land. • The Tamil Nadu State Commission for Women, Chennai recommended and sent the copy of complaint to the Superintendent of Police, Madurai district for action on 05.09.2011. • The National Commission for Scheduled Caste, Chennai sent the action report taken by the Superintendent of Police Madurai district to the victim dated 10.10.2011.
List of documents	1. Patta issued by the Government dated 15.10.2010 with beneficiary list. 2. Copy of FIR in Cr. No.168/2011 dated 25.06.2011. 3. Medical treatment certificate. 4. Copy of complaint by the victim dated 29.06.2011.

	5. Response from National Commission for Scheduled Caste, Chennai dated 15.07.2011. 6. Response from Tamil Nadu State Commission for Women, Chennai dated 05.09.2011.

Source: Evidence Document.

5. Dalit woman Parameswari was abused in caste name, brutally assaulted with weapons and threatened to kill her by the caste Hindu when she opposed for encroaching her land illegally at Vellalakundam Village, Valapadi Taluk, Salem District

Name of the Affected	Parameswari (25)
Religion/caste/sex	Hindu/Arunthathiar/Female
Address	W/o. Mrugaiyan, 252/318, Therkku Thottam, Vellalakundam Village Vazhapadi Taluk Salem District
Incident in Brief	Dalit woman Parameswari (25) W/o. Murugaiyan's land was encroached by caste Hindu Thangaraj and his group when she and her family members intervened and questioned about the land she was abused in caste name and brutally assaulted by the caste Hindus in Vellalakundam Village, Valapadi Taluk, Salem District.
Name of the accused/caste	1. Mr. Thangaraj/Goundar 2. Mr. Duraichami/Goundar 3. Mr. Pakkiam/Goundar and 10 others.
Struggles/Obstacles faced by the victim	• For the past 10 years the victim and her family members were forced to sell the land to the caste Hindus as they need approach pathway to the lands of caste Hindus. • The victim and her family were affected physically and psychologically by the torture of caste Hindus. • Even though complaints were filed against caste Hindu, police did not take action against them. • Till date, the caste Hindus caused annoyance to the victim and her family.
Case registered details	1. Valapadi Police Station Cr.No. 95/2011 u/s 147, 447, 341, 294(b), 379 I.P.C. and 3(1) (x) SC/ST Act, 1989. 2. Valapadi Police Stations Cr.No.157/2011 under sections 147, 323, 506(ii) and 427 IPC and 3(1)

	(x) SC/ST Act, 1989.
Interventions	1. Fact-findings was done by Evidence team on 9.06.2011 2. On 29.06.2011 victim approached Evidence Office directly and supportive counselling was given. 3. Educated the woman victim to understand the laws relating to land rights and stop getting exploited by their opponents. 4. Complaints preferred to National Human Rights Commission, State Human Rights Commission, State Women Commission, Chief Secretary, DGP, ADW SC, District Collector Salem, SP Salem and DSP Valapadi on 30.06.2011 5. Petition under RTI Act was sent to know the stage of the case dated 28.07.2011.
Impact	• Valapadi police had registered FIR in Cr.No.157/11 under IPC section 147, 323, 506(2) IPC r/w 3(1)(10) SC/ST Act. • Accused was arrested by the police. • Strategically we were able to expose in getting justice to the affected by sending various complaints to various Government Departments and Commissions. • Authentic documents were gathered by the team to prosecute the perpetrators. • Due to our assistance the Dalit woman is able to approach the court to seek redress. • The woman victim is now well aware of the laws to reclaim their rights. • Response from National Commission for Scheduled Caste, Chennai for action dated 12.07.2011. • A sum of Rs. 6250 was given as compensation to the victim.
List of Documents	1. Patta issued to the victim 2. Layout sketch 3. Chitta 4. Adangal copy 5. Sale deed to victim's husband Murugayyan dated 24.03.2003. 6. Order of principal District Munsif Salem in I.A.No.1114/2004 in O.S. No.1683/2004 dated 08.11.2004 7. Appeal in C.M.A. No.11/2005 passed by principal Subordinate Judge Salem dated 8.8.2006. 8. Copy of FIR in Cr.No.95/2011 dated 19.01.2011

	9. Copy of FIR in Cr.No.157/2011 dated 30.01.2011 10. Copy of complaint by the victim dated 30.06.2011. 11. Response from National Commission for Scheduled Caste, Chennai dated 12.07.2011. 12. Response from district Adi Dravidar Welfare Department, Salem regarding the compensation dated 30.04.2012.

Source: Evidence Document.

6. Dalit woman Poongavanam was abused in caste name, threatened to kill and assault over the dispute of illegal land grabbing by dominant caste of Thokkavadi Village, Sengam Taluk in Thiruvannamalai District

Name of the Affected	Poongavanam (65)
Religion/caste/sex	Hindu/Parayar/Female
Address	W/o. Chinnadurai, 133,7th ward, Thokkavadi Village Chengam Taluk Thiruvannamalai District
Incident in Brief	Dalit woman Poongavanam (65) W/o. Chinnadurai's 2.48 acres of land was illegally occupied by caste Hindus Chinnathambi and Ayyappan while she resisted for being to take over her land the victim was abused in caste name, assaulted and threatened by the caste Hindu in Thokkavadi Village, Chengam Taluk at Thiruvannamalai District.
Name of the accused/caste	1. Mr. Chinnathambi (35)/Vanniar 2. Mr. Ayyappan (43)/Vanniar
Struggles/obstacles faced by the victim	• Since 2007 the accused has given ill-advised stating that they would assist them to get electricity connection for their land and deceived them by getting a signature from fake documents. • In 2010 when they came back to their home town after a long gap they found that it was registered falsely in the name of the dominant caste. • When they objected over the disputed land they were assaulted, threatened and abused in caste name. • Following the complaints from the victim the accused were not arrested but bail granted from the High Court.

	• Though the victim has proper document from the government stating that her panchami land cannot be transferred or sold to others, still it is a dream to own a land for the victim.
Case registered details	Chengam Police Station Cr.No.1048/2010 under section 427, 506(ii) I.P.C. and 3(1) (x) SC/ST Act, 1989 on 19.12.2010.
Interventions	1. Fact-findings was done by Evidence team on 2.06.2011. 2. Educated the woman victim to understand the laws relating to land rights violations and stop getting exploited by their opponents. 3. Complaints preferred to State Human Rights Commission, National SC/ST Commission, State Women Commission, Chief Secretary, DGP, ADW SC, District Collector Thiruvannamalai District, SP Thiruvannamalai, and DSP Chengam on 18.06.2011. 4. Petition was sent under RTI Act to the Public Information Officer-cum-Additional Superintendent of Police, Thiruvannamalai to know the stage of the case.
Impact	• Chengam police had registered FIR in Cr.No. 1048/10 under IPC section 427, 506(1) r/w 3(1) (10) SC/ST Act. • Authentic documents were gathered by the team to prosecute the perpetrators. • Due to our assistance the Dalit woman is able to approach the legal system to seek redress. • The woman victim is now well aware of the laws to reclaim their rights related to land. • Response from National Commission for Scheduled Caste, Chennai for action dated 22.06.2011. • Reply under RTI Act was received on 19.08.2011. • PRC 10/11 is pending with the Court of Judicial Magistrate, Chengam. • Following our complaint in regard to assault case a sum of Rs. 6250 was given to the victim as compensation on 09.12.2012.
List of documents	1. Sale deed dated 10.05.1989 2. Sale agreement dated 3.11.97 3. Layout sketch 4. Encumbrance certificate dated 30.06.2010. 5. Land tax receipts 6. Copy of FIR in Cr.No.1048/2010 dated 19.12.2010. 7. Copy of complaint by Poongavanam dated 18.06.2011. 8. Response from National Commission for Scheduled Caste, Chennai dated 22.06.2011.

	9. Response from Tamil Nadu State Commission for Women, Chennai dated 29.06.2011. 10. Reply under RTI Act dated 23.08.2011.

Source: Evidence Documents.

7. Dalit couple Muniammal and Rasu allege confiscation of land by caste Hindu moneylender for 16 years in Vadaputhupatti Village, Periakulam Taluk, Theni District

Name of the Affected	Muniymmal (43)
Religion/caste/sex	Hindu/Arunthathiar/Female
Address	171231, M.G.R Nagar, Vadaputhupatti Village Annanji Post, Periakulam Taluk Theni District
Incident in Brief	Dalit woman Muniammal (55) and her husband Rasu a resident of Vadaputhupatti Village, Periakulam Taluk at Theni District alleged that a caste Hindu moneylender had taken possession of their house and abused them even after they were willing to clear the debt.
Name of the accused/caste	1. Mr. Selvam (45)/Kallar 2. Mr. Mayee (40)/Kallar 3. Ms. Maheswari (35)/Kallar
Struggles/Obstacles faced by the victim	• The victim and her family members were struggling for 10 years to recover their property. • False case was registered against the victim by producing a fake document that the victim had borrowed one lakh rupee instead of actual amount of Rs. 13,000. • The couple also found that the trees belonging to them for 16 years were being felled by the accused. • When questioned the victim and her family members were threatened of dire consequences. • Right now the victim had erected a small hut near their relative's house as they could not occupy due to unauthorized occupant of the caste Hindus.
Case registered details	Allinagaram Police Station Cr.No. 210/2011 u/s 427, 506(ii) I.P.C. and 3(1) (x) SC/ST Act, 1989 dated 28.06.2011.

Interventions	1. On 06.08.2011, team of Evidence went to the spot and undertook fact-finding. 2. On 08.08.2011 press release was given to highlight the issue to the public. 3. On 11.08.2011, victim and her family members directly reported to the office. 4. Supportive counselling was given to the victim. 5. On the same day complaint was prepared on behalf of the victim. 6. On 11.08.2011, complaint was sent to the Human Rights Commission, Govt. authorities and Police Officials for appropriate action. 7. On 08.09.2011 follow-up petition was sent to National SC/ST Commission. 8. On 14.11.2011 petition under RTI Act was sent to SP Theni to know the present status of the case.
Impact	• On 28.06.2011 Allinagaram Police Station had registered FIR in Cr.No.210/11 u/s 427, 506(i), IPC r/w 3(1) (10) SC/ST Act. • On 09.08.2011, news published in English daily *Hindu* and 11.07.2011 *Indian Express.* • On 19.08.2011 reply letter received from National SC/ST Commission. • On 08.12.2011 reply under RTI was received. • PRC No. 7/2012 pending with Judicial Magistrate Theni.
List of Documents	1. House site patta issued to the victim 2. House tax receipts 3. Copy of FIR in Cr.No.210/2011 dated 28.06.2011. 4. Press release dated 08.08.2011. 5. Paper clipping 6. Copy of complaint by the victim dated 11.08.2011.

Source: Evidence Documents.

8. Dalit woman Mayakkal and her family members were abused in caste name, assaulted and intimidated by the caste Hindu with intention of encroaching victim's land illegally in Poomparai Village, Kodaikanal Taluk, Dindigul District

Name of the Affected	Mayakkal (35)
Religion/caste/sex	Hindu/Arunthathiar/female

Address	2/420, Vayavali Street, Poomparai Village, Poomparai Post, Kodaikanal Taluk, Dindigul District.
Incident in Brief	Dalit woman Mayakkal (35) W/o. Murugan, a resident of Poomparai Village, Kodaikanal Taluk at Dindigul District and her family members were abused in caste name and assaulted brutally with deadly weapons and threatened to murder them by caste Hindu Subramaniyam and his gang while they confronted them against illegal encroachment of their land.
Name of the accused/caste	1. Mr. Subramni (60)/Servai 2. Mr. Murugan (35)/Servai 3. Mr. Balu (38)/Servai 4. Mr. Sambayee (55)/Servai 5. Mr. Thanapal (35)/Servai and others
Struggles/obstacles faced by the victim	• Delay in filing FIR after request. • Brutal assault on the family members and injured. • Constant humiliation, life threat and fear. • Repeated attack by caste Hindu even after filing FIR and intimidating over illegally land grabbing from the victim. • The victim was forced to stay outside the village due to constant threat even after having a patta land with ownership right. • Due to the recent brutal assaults the victim got admitted in the government hospital for one week and due to fear of life her husband was forced to get discharge from the hospital. • Loss of family income during the incident and the crops were destroyed from their land. • Due to this incident her children could not pursue their studies. • Worst humiliation was that the water source owned by the victim was polluted by human feces.
Case registered details	Kodaikanal Police Station Cr. No. 403/2011 under Section 147, 294(b), 427 and 506(i) I.P.C. and 3(1) (x), 3(1) (13) SC/ST Act, 1989 on 20.07.2011.
Interventions	1. On 16.07.2011, victim reported to Evidence office directly. 2. Supportive counselling was given to the victim. 3. Complaint preferred to State Human Rights Commission, National SC/ST Commission,

	Chief Secretary, DGO, ADW SC, District Collector Dindigul, SP Dindigul, DSP Kodaikanal on 18.07.2011 4. On 9.07.2011 team of Evidence along with victim went to meet SP Dindigul to give complaint. 5. On 25.07.2011 press release was given highlighting the news to the public. 6. On 14.11.2011 petition under RTI was sent to SP Dindigul to know the present status of the case. 7. Petition was sent to the District Collector, Dindigul for compensation to the victim.
Impact	• On 20.07.2011 Kodaikanal Police had registered FIR in Cr.No. 403/2011 u/s 147, 294(b), 427, 506(i), IPC r/w 3(1) (13) SC/ST Act. • Response received from National Commission for Scheduled Castes, Chennai on 21.07.2011. • Response received from State Human Rights Commission, Chennai on 26.07.2011. • On 26.07.2011 and 27.07.2011 news was published in *Indian Express* and *Deccan Chronicle*. • Response received from Women Commission, Chennai on 12.09.2011. • 13.12.2011 reply under RTI was received. • PRC No. 11/2011 is pending in JM Court, Kodaikanal.
List of Documents	1. Patta issued to the victim's husband Murugan. 2. Land tax receipt. 3. Wound certificate issued for the victim, victim's husband. 4. Copy of complaint by the victim dated 16.07.2011. 5. Copy of FIR Cr.No. 403/2011 dated 20.07.2011. 6. Response from the National Commission for Scheduled Caste Chennai dated 21.07.2011. 7. Press release dated 25.07.2011. 8. Paper clipping in the *Indian Express* and *Deccan Chronicle* dated 26.07.2011 and 27.07.2011. 9. Response received from the State Human Rights Commission, Chennai dated 26.07.2011. 10. Response received from the Tamil Nadu State Commission for Women, Chennai dated 05.09.2011. 11. Reply under RTI Act dated 13.12.2011. 12. Petition to District Collector dated 11.05.2012. for compensation.

Sources: Evidence Documents.

9. Dalit woman Veerammal was abused in caste name, assaulted and threatened over illegal land encroachment by caste Hindus in Kodangipatti Village, Ottanchatiram Taluk, Dindigul District

Name of the Affected	Veerammal (56)
Religion/caste/sex	Hindu/Arunthathiar/Female
Address	276/3, Ambedkar Colony, Kodangipatti Village, Kodangipatti Post, Ottanchatiram Taluk, Dindigul District.
Incident in Brief	Dalit woman Veerammal (56) W/o. Velan (late) a resident of Kodangipatti Village, Ottanchatiram Taluk at Dindigul District was abused in caste name and brutally assaulted by caste Hindu Natarajan @ Palleri when she intervened and questioned about her land being encroached by them.
Name of the accused/caste	1. Mr. Natarajan@ Palleri (65)/Goundar
Struggles/Obstacles faced by the victim	• The caste Hindus objected her not to cultivate the land and forced her to allot piece of land to the temple of caste Hindus when she objected the victim and her relatives were beaten up. • She went to the Police Station to prefer complaint on her own but no proper response from the police. • On the other hand she had legal battle in the Court for more than 7 years to claim her land right and got favourable order in the year 1993. Though she got the court order she could retrieve her land back but due to Evidence's intervention in the month of October 2011 she got back her lands.
Case registered details	No cases were registered as Dindigul Superintendent of Police directly made an enquiry and handed over the land to the affected after a long battle.
Interventions	1. On 26.07.2011 victim Veerammal and her family members directly reported to the office. 2. Supportive counselling was given to the victim. 3. On the same day complaint was prepared on behalf of the victim. 4. Complaint referred to State Human Rights. Commission, National SC/ST Commission,

	State Women Commission, Chief Secretary, DGP, ADW SC, District Collector Dindigul, SP Dindigul, DSP Ottanchatiram, RDO Ottanchatiram and Inspector Edaiyakottai on 27.07.2011
Impact	• On 04.08.2011 response received from State Human Rights Commission, Chennai. • On 17.08.2011 response received from the National Commission for Scheduled Castes, Chennai. • Due to intervention of Evidence on month of October 2011 District Superintendent of Police, Dindigul made an enquiry and victim Veerammal's land was retrieved from the Hindus. • We have succeeded in reclaiming the 18 acres of 5 Dalit families' land along with the victim (3 acres is her share) after 25 years of struggles. The victim was able to continue to do her agricultural work in her retrieved land.
List of Documents	7. Copy of order in appeal no. 24/96 dated 29.06.2001. 8. Copy of complaint by the victim dated 26.07.2011. 9. Response received from State Human Rights Commission, Chennai dated 04.08.2011 10. Response received from National Commission for Scheduled Caste, Chennai dated 17.08.2011.

Sources: Evidence Documents.

10. Dalit woman Lakshmi was abused in caste name and intimidated to kill her by dominant caste when objected to the illegal encroachment of her house site in Periakalayam Puthur Village, Palani Taluk in Dindigul District

Name of the Affected	Lakshmi (50)
Religion/caste/sex	Hindu/Arunthathiar/Female
Address	W/o. Murugesan, 25, Mathari Street, Periakalayam Puthur Village, Neikkarapatti Town Panchayat, Palani Taluk, Dinndigul District

Incident in Brief	Dalit woman Lakshmi (50) W/o. Murugeasan a resident of Periyakalayamputhur Village, Palani Taluk at Dindigul District was abused in caste name and threatened to murder by caste Hindus, when she showed objection over the illegal encroachment of her house site.
Name of the accused/caste	1. Mr. Murugan (45)/Goundar 2. Mr. Mayandi (40)/Goundar 3. Mr. Abuthakir (40)/Muslim 4. Ms. Acharammal (50)/Goundar
Struggles/Obstacles faced by the victim	• Since two months in 2011 the victim and her family members were facing risk for their life to get back their lost land. • Police refused to accept the victim's complaint indirectly favouring the caste Hindus. • Police pressurized the woman victim to drop her case or to accept a "compromise" after restoring the land instead of proper action. • No proper legal guidance was given to the victim to restore back her lost land.
Case registered details	The victim preferred and her complaint in Palani Taluk Police Station.
Interventions	1. Victim Lakshmi and her family members directly approached Evidence Office on 21.05.2011. 2. Supportive counselling was given to the affected. 3. The former local trained activist of Evidence was identified and was asked to accompany the affected victim to meet the officials. 4. Educate the woman victim to understand the laws relating to land violations and stop getting by their opponent. 5. Complaints preferred to State Human Rights Commission, National SC/ST Commission, State Women Commission, Chief Secretary, DGP, ADW SC, Superintendent of Police, DSP, Inspector and RDO on 21.05.2011. 6. Petition under RTI Act was sent to the Public Information Officer-cum-Additional Superintendent of Police, Dindigul to know the stage of the case, on 01.08.2011.
Impact	• Tamil Nadu State Women Commission and National Commission for Scheduled Castes, State Human Rights Commission forwarded to Superintendent of Police to look into this matter. • State Human Rights Commission, Chennai forwarded copy of complaint to the Superintendent of Police, Dindigul for necessary action. • The National Commission for Scheduled Caste,

	Chennai forwarded copy of complaint to the Superintendent of Police, Dindigul for taking action on the allegation of the victim. • Authentic documents were gathered by the team to prosecute the perpetrators. • Due to our assistance the Dalit woman was able to approach the legal system to seek justice. • The victim felt secured and motivated to take up the issue illegally. • After our repeated intervention and follow-up the affected got back her lost land after police enquiry. • The woman victim is now well aware of the laws to reclaim their rights related to land.
List of documents	1. Copy of the patta in the name of victim's mother Makaliammal. 2. Adangal account copy. 3. Land tax receipts. 4. Forged sale deed. 5. Copy of complaint by Karuppammmal dated 17.05.2011. 6. Response from Tamil Nadu State Commission for Women, Chennai dated 27.05.2011.

Source: Evidence Documents.

11. Dalit woman Ms. Alagumeena and her community members were abused in caste name, assaulted and intimidated by a dominant caste over the ownership of a temple land in Manjampatti Village in Madurai District

Name of the Affected	Alagumeena (55)
Religion/Caste/Sex	Hindu/Parayar/Female
Address	W/o. Solai Alagan, Manjampatti Colony, Manjampatti Village, Chatrapatti Post, Madurai North Taluk, Madurai District
Incident in Brief	Dalit woman victim Alagumeena and her community members were abused in caste name, brutally assaulted, threatened and intimidated. Foisted a false case against the victim and her community people for claiming a temple land from the caste Hindu in Manjampatti Village, in Madurai District

Name of the accused/caste	1. Mr. Rajamni (60)/Goundar
Struggles/Obstacles faced by the victim	• Though Dalit woman Alagumeena and 34 Dalits were falsely implicated and imprisoned they fought to retrieve their temple land against the caste Hindus. • Perpetrator foisting false police cases against the affected to pressurize them to drop their legitimate cases. • Dalit villagers were ostracized and forced to stay out of their village by caste Hindus. • Though the Dalit are having proper documents to claim the ownership of Karuppanasami temple land till now they are not in a position to enjoy and fighting endlessly to retrieve the temple land.
Case registered details	Oomachikulam M. Chatrapatti police registered FIR in Cr.No. 379/2011 under section 323, 294(b),506(i) I.P.C. and 4 of Tamil Nadu Woman Harassment Act read with 3(1) (x) SC/ST Act, 1989 on 09.05.2011.
Interventions	1. Fact-finding was done by team of Evidence on 07.05.2011. 2. Supportive and educative counselling was given to affected victim. 3. Sensitized the rural Dalit woman to be familiar with the laws relating to land rights. 4. Complaints were sent to State Human Rights Commission, National SC/ST Commission, State Women Commission, Chief Secretary, DGP, ADW SC, District Collector, Madurai Superintendent of Police on 23.05.2011. 5. Case was filed before the High Court, Madurai bench for seeking order to receive the land and file the charge sheet against the accused on 06.08.2011 and its pending.
Impact	• Oomachikulam M. Chatrapatti police had registered FIR in Cr. No. 379/11 under the IPC section 323, 294(b), 506(i) r/w 4 of TNWH Act, 3(1) (10) SC/ST Act on 09.05.2011. • Authentic documents were gathered by the team to prosecute the perpetrators. • Due to our assistance the Dalit woman is able to approach the Court to seek redressals. • Due to our intervention, continuous psychological support and follow-up to the affected and the community members, they showed courage and confidence. The initiative

	was to help them to overcome from the feeling of fear and insecurity. • Strategically our interventions were able to expose the violations. In order to get justice on behalf of the affected various complaints were sent to various Government Departments and Commissions for immediate action. • The woman victim is now well aware of the laws to reclaim their rights related to land.
List of documents	1. Patta for temple land 2. Chitta 3. Adangal account 4. Copy of trust deed in the name of Dalit Alagan 5. Petition to the EB for electricity connection in the name of Dalit Alagan. 6. Copy of FIR in Cr. No. 379/2011 dated 09.05.2011. 7. Copy of complaints by the victim Alagumeena dated 21.05.2011.

Source: Evidence Documents.

12. Dalit woman Shanthi (32) and 57 Dalit women beneficiaries of Government allotted land were not distributed Patta due to the negligence of the local administration at Perumparai Village, Athur Taluk, Dindigul District

Name of the affected	Shanthi (43)
Religion/caste/sex	Hindu/Pallan/Female
Address	W/o. Ganeshan M.G.R. Nagar, Perumparai Village, Perumparai Post, Atur Taluk, Dindigul District
Incident in Brief	Dalit woman Shanthi and other 57 Dalits families were allotted with land under TADHCO SCHEME during the year 2006-2009, but till now the land has not been measured and patta distributed officials were hassled by the administration in Perumparai Village in Athur Taluk at Dindigul District.
Name of the accused/caste	—
Struggles/Obstacles faced by the victim	• Though the beneficiaries are women under Tamil Nadu Adi Dravidar Housing and Development Corporation (TADCHO) land purchase scheme meant for women

	beneficiaries were not given patta allotted for them since 2007. • Women are abstained from engaging in farm activity or agriculture and not aware of which is their own piece of land. • The women were shocked to get notice from the bank to repay the amount with interest without issuing a patta or without getting any benefit from the land. • Allotted land could not be measured as it will not serve any useful purpose without measurement and loan waived.
Case registered details	The High Court Madurai bench directed the District Collector, Dindigul to send the explanation report within one week on this matter.
Interventions	1. On 2.11.2010 victim approached Evidence office directly. 2. Supportive counselling was given to the victim and her family. 3. On 2.11.2010 case was filed before Madras High Court, Madurai bench. 4. On 15.12.2010 Evidence team along with the victim met the bank officials and lodged a complaint. 5. On 24.01.2012 press news was given to highlight the news to the public. 6. Copy of complaint addressed Mr. Chellappan former, and Member of National Commission for Scheduled Castes, Chennai dated 24.01.2012
Impact	On 03.01.2012 news was published in *Dinamalar* which revealed that Madras High Court bench ordered District Collector Dindigul for action. Athoor Thasildhar issued patta to Ms. Shanthi and 3 other beneficiaries On 2.02.2012 news was published in English daily.
List of documents	1. Patta issued to the victim Shanthi and 4 other Dalit women only. 2. Petition by which addressed to State Bank of India, Madurai for cancellation of bank loan dated 12.10.2010. 3. Copy of petition by the victim to the District Collector, Dindigul dated 10.10.2010. 4. Press release dated 24.10.2012. 5. Copy of the complaint by the victim dated 24.10.2012. 6. Paper clipping dated 2.2.2012.

Source: Evidence Documents.

13. Dalit Swaminathan's land could not be retrieved after lease period when it is claimed they were abused in caste name, assaulted and threatened for filing the case in the court by the caste Hindu at Devinaickanpatti Village, Vedasandur Taluk, Dindigul District

Name of the Affected	Swaminathan (37)
Religion/Caste/Sex	Hindu/Arunthathiar/Female
Address	X/2, Colony Street, Devinaikanpatti Village, Devinaikanpatti Post, Kasipalayam via, Vedasandur Taluk, Dindigul District.
Incident in Brief	Dalit victim Swaminathan (37) S/o. Veeran a resident of Devinaikanpatti Village, Vedasandur Taluk, Dindigul District and his wife Palaniammal were abused in caste name, slapped with foot-wear and threatened to murder if the victim fail to withdraw case which was pending in the Court regarding a land dispute.
Name of the accused/caste	1. Mr. Chellappan Goundar (70)/Goundar 2. Ms. Pappathi (62)/Goundar 3. Mr. Eswaran (42)/Goundar
Struggles/Obstacles faced by the victim	• It was nine years of struggle to get back the ownership of their own patta land the caste Hindu who is falsely claiming the land. • Frequent visit to Court and enquiry had to mental stress and unnecessary expenses. • To live under constant threat living with sleepless night. • The victim approached the Court to retrieve land. Even after, the victim faced annoyance to withdraw the case by the caste Hindu.
Case registered details	No case was registered as the case was pending in the Civil Court and case considered as civil dispute.
Interventions	1. On 27.07.2011 victim directly reported to Evidence office. 2. Supportive counselling was given to the victim and his family members. 3. Complaint preferred to State Human Rights Commission, National SC/ST Commission, State Women Commission, Chief Secretary, DGP, ADW SC, District Collector Dindigul, SP

	Dindigul, DSP Vedasandur, Vedasandur Police Station and RDO Palani on 10.11.2011. 4. On 3.1.2011 petition under RTI Act was sent to SP Dindigul to know the present status of the case.
Impact	• Response received from National SC/ST Commission, Chennai forwarded letter to Superintendent of Police to take necessary action on 21.11.2011. • Strategically we were able to expose in getting justice to the affected by sending various complaints to various Government Departments and Commissions. • Authentic documents were obtained by the team to prosecute the perpetrators. • Due to our assistance the Dalit woman was able to approach the Court to seek redressal. • The woman victim is now well aware of the laws to reclaim their rights related to land.
List of Documents	1. Land tax receipt 2. Lease document dated 03.12.1991 3. Copy of complaints by the victim dated 10.11.2011. 4. Response received from National Commission for Scheduled Caste, Chennai dated 21.11.2011.

Source: Evidence Documents.

14. Dalit Murugan's two brothers married to caste Hindus women exploiting the situation the power of attorney of the land used by caste Hindu while objected the affected power was abused in caste name and intimidated at Kallimandayam Village, Ottanchatiram Taluk, Dindigul District

Name of the Affected	Murugan (34)
Religion/Caste/Sex	Hindu/Aruhrathiyar/Male
Address	K.K. Nagar, Kallimandayam Village, Oddanchatriam Taluk Dindigul District
Brief of the incident	Dalit victim Murugan (34) S/o, Maran (late) a resident of K.K. Nagar, Kallimandayam, Dindigul district alleged to have exploited the marriage of two brothers from Dalit community who married

	caste Hindu women was usurped by the caste Hindu and had power of attorney for their land in the caste Hindu name.
Name of the accused/caste	1. Mr. Nachimuthu (68)/Goundar
Struggles/Obstacles faced by the victim	• The victim's two elder brothers fell in love and married caste Hindu girls and so they were forced to leave the native place leaving their own land since 2002. • Till now the caste Hindus are threatening not to enter their native place stating that it was intercaste marriage in order to grab their lands. • Though the victim cancelled the power of attorney which is in the name of Nachimuthu Goundar went worthless. • Past eight years they are not getting any economic benefit from the lost 12 acres of land. • No proper action or response from the Kallimandayam Police Station even after preferring complaint in the year 2006 only the receipt was given no FIR was registered. • The officials are considering this as civil case and disposing the case without proper action.
Case registered details	Kaliimandayam police issued receipt no. 78 dated 03.11.2006.
Interventions	1. On 11.08.2011 victim Murugan and his family members directly reported to Evidence office. 2. Support counselling was given to the victim. 3. Sensitized the rural Dalit woman to get familiar about the laws relating to land rights, violations and stop getting exploited by their opponents. 4. Complaints preferred to State Human Rights Commission, National SC/ST Commission, State Women Commission, Chief Secretary, DGP, ADW SC, District Collector, SP Dindigul, DSP Ottanchatiram, RDO Palani, and Inspector Kallimandayam on 12.08.2011. 5. On 13.08.2011press news was sent to media release was given to highlight the issue to the public. 6. On 17.11.2011 petition under RTI was sent to the SP Dindigul to know the present status of the case. 7. Case was filed before the High Court, Madurai bench to seeking order to register FIR u/s 3(1) (10) SC/ST Act, 1989 and to retrieve the land.

Impact	• On 14.08.2011 news was published in English daily *Indian Express* and 15.08.2011 in *Deccan Chronicle*. • On 26.08.2011 reply letter received from RDO Palani, Dindigul district.
List of Documents	1. Patta (8) issued to the victim 2. Land tax receipt 3. Sale deed to the victim dated 27.05.1964. 4. Sale deed to the victim dated 21.08.1967. 5. Power of attorney given to the caste Hindu dated 28.01.2004. 6. Cancellation documents for power of attorney dated 18.07.2006. 7. Sale deed dated 12.02.2004-11.02.2006. 8. Complaints to the Kallimandayam police dated 03.11.2006. 9. Receipts issued by police dt.3.11.2006. 10. Copy of complaint by the victim dated 12.08.2011. 11. Press release dated 13.08.2011. 12. Paper clippings. 13. Letter of RDO Palani to Dy. Superintendent of Police Ottanchatiram dated 26.08.2011. 14. Encumbrance certificate dated 06.09.2011.

Source: Evidence Documents.

15. Dalit Devesahayam and his family members were abused in caste name and committed criminal intimidation by the caste Hindu when the victim objected the illegal encroachment of land at Jedarpalayam, Paramathi—Vellore Taluk, Namakkal District

Name of the Affected	Devasahayam (65)
Religion/Caste/Sex	Hindu/Parayar/Male
Address	S/o. Kittan (late), 4/168A, North Street, Jedarpalayam Village. Jedarpalayam Post, Paramathi—Vellore Taluk, Nammakkal District.
Incident in Brief	Dalit Devesahayam (65) S/o. Kittan a resident of Jedarpalayam Village, Paramathi—Velore Taluk, Namakkal District was abused in the caste name, attempt to assault and threatened to murder by caste Hindu Valathigoundar and his gang when he intervened and questioned about the illegal encroachment of his land by the caste Hindu.

Name of the accused/caste	1. Mr. Valathigoundar (60)/Goundar 2. Mr. Muthuvel (48)/Goundar 3. Mr. Subramani (39)/Goundar
Struggles/Obstacles faced by the victim	• The victim continuously fought against the caste Hindu's annoyance and encroachment of his own patta land.
Case registered details	Jedarpalayam Police Station Cr. No. 261/2011 under sections 506(ii) IPC and 3(1) (x) SC/ST Act, 1989.
Interventions	1. On 16.07.2011 victim directly reported to Evidence office. 2. Supportive counselling was given to them. 3. Complaint preferred to State Human Rights Commission, National SC/ST Commission, and Chief Secretary, DGP, ADW SC, District Collector Namakkal, DSP Paramathivelore and RDO Thiruchenkodu on 17.7.2011. 4. Petition under RTI Act was sent to know the stage of the case on 16.05.2012.
Impact	• On 21.07.2011 Jedarpalayam Police Station had registered in the FIR in Cr. No. 261/2011 u/s 506(ii), IPC r/w 3(1) (10) SC/ST Act. • Strategically we were able to expose in getting justice to the affected by sending various complaints to various Government Departments and Commissions. • Authentic documents were gathered by the team to prosecute the perpetrators • Due to our assistance the Dalit woman was able to approach the legal system to seek redress. • The women victim is now well aware of the laws to reclaim their rights related to land. • On 16.08.2011 National Commission for Scheduled Castes, Chennai forwarded a letter to Superintendent of Police, Namakkal to take necessary action.
List of Documents	1. Patta issued to victim's wife Pakialakshmi. 2. Layout map for S.No. 758/A/4. 3. Land tax receipt. 4. Copy of police receipt No. 90/2011 dated 10.07.2011. 5. Copy of complaints by the victim dated 16.07.2011. 6. Response from National Commission for Scheduled Castes, Chennai dated 16.08.2011.

Source: Evidence Documents.

16. Dalit Asirvatham's land was encroached legally and buried a dead body by the caste Hindu when objected he was abused in caste name and intimidated to kill at Jedarpalayam Village, P. Vellore Taluk, Namakkal District

Name of the affected	Asirvatham (39)
Religion/Caste/Sex	Hindu/Parayar/Female
Address	Door No. 4/168 A, North Street Jedarpalayam Village Tiruchengode (Via) P. Vellore Taluk Namakkal District
Incident in Brief	Dalit Asirvatham (39) S/o. Devasakayam, a resident of Jedarpalayam Village, Paramathi Vellore Taluk of Namakkal District was abused in caste name and threatened to murder by caste Hindu while they opposed to bury the dead body of caste Hindu Valathikounder in the victim's land.
Name of the accused/caste	1. Mr. Sadhasivam (32)/Gounder 2. Mr. Sakthivel (49) Goundar
Struggles/Obstacles faced by the victim	• Humiliating the victim by burying a dead body in the victim's land. • Right to live is denied since 2011. • Abusing the victim and her family members in filthy language lost their self-respect. • Officials were favouring the caste Hindus. • Following the incident other 6 Dalit families' houses were demolished mistakenly thoroughly in the pretext of evacuating the lands. Purposefully they have demolished and officials regretted. • Constant threat to the victim.
Case registered details	Jedarpalayam Police Station Cr.No. 261/2011 under section 506(ii) I.P.C and 3(I) (x) SC/ST Act, 1989.
Interventions	1. On 08.08.2011, Victim Asirvatham and his family members directly reported to Evidence office. 2. Supportive counselling was given to them. 3. Complaint preferred to State Human Rights Commission, National SC/ST Commission, Chief Secretary, DGP, ADW SC, District Collector Namakkal, SP Namakkal, DSP Paramathivellore, RDO Thiruchenkodu, and Inspector Paramathivellore on 09.08.2011. 4. On 10.08.2011 Press news was sent to media to highlight the news to public.

	5. Petition under RTI Act was sent to know the stage of the case on 16.05.2012.
Impact	• On 21.07.2011 Jedarpalayam Police had registered FIR in Cr.No. 261/2011 u/s 506(ii), IPC and 3(I)(10) SC/ST Act. • Victim's family members were strengthened, encouraged and motivated to speak and take up the issue. • Authentic documents were gathered by the team to prosecute the perpetrators.
List of Documents	1. House tax receipts. 2. Copy of complaint by the victim dated 09.08.2011.

Source: *Voices of Dalit Victim—Land Rights Violation: People's Tribunal for Legal Reddressal*, Madurai: Evidence, 2012.

17. Dalit Dhaniselvam was murdered by the caste Hindu when refused to sell the allotted house at Kaungamuthanpatti Village, Uthamapalayam Taluk

Name of the Affected	Dhaniselvam (deceased)
Religion/Caste/Sex	Hindu/Parayar/Male
Address	Saravanan (24) 182, Mariamman Koil Street, Karugamuthanpatti Village Karugamuthanpatti Post Uthamapalayam Taluk Theni District
Incident in Brief	Deceased Dalit Thaniselvam (52) a resident of Karungamuthanpatti Village at Theni District was brutally murdered by a caste Hindu over land dispute.
Name of the accused/caste	1. Mr. Eswaran (42)/Piramalai Kallar 2. Mr. Paramasivam (48)/Piramalai Kallar
Struggles/Obstacles faced by the victim	• The deceased victim had sacrificed his life to save precious house site. • Prior to the death of the deceased many petitions were sent to CM Cell, District SP, Collector and personal visit to Chief Secretary Chennai stating that his life was under threat but no proper action taken to save his life. • He was the sole person who fought to retain the house site (Thokkuppu Veedu).

Case Registered details	Cumbum South police registered FIR Cr.No. 240/2011 under sections 341, 302 I.P.C r/w 3(2) (v) SC/ST Act, 1989 on 04.12.2011.
Interventions	• On 03.01.2012 deceased victim Thaniselvam's family members directly reported to the office of Evidence. • Supportive counselling was given to victim. • Complaint was sent to State Human Rights Commission, National SC/ST Commission, Chief Secretary, DGP, ADW SC, District Collector Theni, SP Theni, DSP Uthamapalayam, Inspector, Cumbum on 03.01.2012. • Petition under RTI Act was sent to know the present stage of case on 20.02.2012. • Petition sent on 26.04.2010 to the District Collector, Theni for giving compensation to the victim's legal heir.
Impact	• On 04.12.2012 Cumbum South Police Station had registered FIR in Cr.No. 240/2011 U/s 341, 302, IPC and 3(2)(5) SC/ST Act. • Accused was arrested by the police. • PRC.No. 21/2012 is pending in the Court. • Response from SHRC Chennai dated 23.01.2012. • Response received from National Commission for Scheduled Caste, Chennai on 16.02.2012. • Deceased victim's family members were strengthened, encouraged and motivated to speak and take up the issue. • Authentic documents were gathered by the team to prosecute the perpetrators. • Reply under RTI Act was received on 09.03.2012.
List of Documents	1. Copy of FIR in Cr.No. 240/2011 dated 04.12.2011. 2. Post-mortem certificate dated 30.12.2011 3. Copy of complaint by the deceased victim's son Saravanan dated 03.01.2012. 4. Response from SHRC dated 23.01.2012. 5. Response from National Commission for SC dated 16.02.2012. 6. Reply under RTI Act dated 09.03.2012.

Source: Evidence Documents.

18. Dalit Rajagopal's land was illegally grabbed with forged documents by a Muslim and when objected victim was abused in caste name and threatened to kill by a caste Hindu land care-taker at Sedapatti Village Periyakulam Taluk, Theni District

Name of the Affected	Rajagopal (65)
Religion/Caste/Sex	Hindu/Parayar/Male
Address	S/o. Kanthan @ Kandasamy 13-5-75, Valluvar Colony Street, Sedapatti Village, Vadugapatti Post, Periyakulam Taluk, Theni District
Incident in Brief	Dalit victim Rajagopal's land was illegally grabbed by Nazimudhin and his group when he objected he was abused in caste name and threaten to kill in Sedapatti village, Periyakulam Taluk, Theni District
Name of the accused/caste	1. Mr. Amanullah/Muslim 2. Ms. Hussainia Parveen/Muslim 3. Mr. Devaraj (50) Kallar
Struggles/Obstacles faced by the victim	• The Dalit victim faced threats by the influential Muslims and caste Hindu for illegal grabbing of his land by showing forged documents. • Police refused to file FIR against the dominant caste even after preferred complaint on illegal grabbing. • Denied ownership for the victim even after having authentic documents. • Loss of trees worth Rs. 25,000 was uprooted by the caste Hindus.
Case registered details	Receipt issued by Thenkarai Police in R.No. 596/2011 dated 25.09.2011.
Interventions	1. On 18.10.2011 team of Evidence went the spot and undertook fact-finding. 2. On the same day sworn statement recorded which was given by the victim. 3. On 14.12.2011 victim directly reported to the office. 4. Supportive counseling was given to the victim. 5. On the same day complaint was prepared on behalf of the victim. 6. On 15.12.2011 complaint was sent to the Human Rights Commission, Govt. authorities and Police Officials for appropriate action. 7. On 17.02.2012, petition under RTI Act was sent to know the stage of the case.

Impact	• On 26.12.2011 reply letter received from National SC/ST Commission. • Strategically we were able to expose in getting justice to the affected by sending various complaints to various government mechanisms and Commissions. • Authentic documents were gathered by the team to prosecute the perpetrators. • Due to our assistance the Dalit victim was able to approach the legal system to seek redress. • The Dalit victim is now well aware of the laws to reclaim their rights related to land.
List of Documents	1. False patta issued to the accused. 2. Adangal in the name of victim's father Kandan. 3. Chitta for victims's father Kandan. 4. Land tax receipts. 5. Forged power of attorney. 6. Forged sale deed dated 19.04.2000 S.No. 1071/3B. 7. Forged sale deed dated 19.04.2000 S.No. 3118. 8. Petition by P. Kandasamy for pension dated 23.07.2004. 9. Petition by the victim Rajagopal to Thenkarai police dt.24.09.2011. 10. Receipt issued by Thenkarai Periakulam police dated 25.09.2011. 11. Encumbrance certificate for S.No. 1071/3B and 3118/1 dt 02.12.2011. 12. Copy of complaint by the victim dated 15.12.2011. 13. Response from National Commission for SC dated 26.12.2011.

Source: Evidence Documents.

19. Dalit Ramakrishnan's (differently abled person) house was illegally occupied and when objected he was abused in caste name and threatened to murder by the caste Hindu at Kottakulam Village, Senkottai Taluk, Thirunelveli District

Name of the Affected	Ramakrishnan (42)
Religion/Caste/Sex	Hindu/Parayar/male
Address	S/o. Thangavel (Lane) 324, R.C. Colony Street, Kottakulam Village, Kottakulam Post, Senkottai Taluk Thirunelveli District

Incident in Brief	Dalit visually differently-abled person Ramakrishnan house was illegally occupied by caste Hindu Kalyani and his wife Vasantha when he objected he was abused in caste name and threatened to kill in Kottakulam Village, Senkottai Taluk, Thirunelveli District
Name of the accused/caste	1. Mr. Kalyani (55) Moopanar 2. Ms. Vasantha (49) Moopanar
Struggles/Obstacles faced by the victim	• Though Dalit victim visually differently-abled person was living under constant fear and lost his own house due to the intimidation of the caste Hindu, faced and fought against them. • The caste Hindus had exploited the situation as he belongs to Dalit community and differently-abled person. • No proper person to extend legal help to approach the police.
Case registered details	Matter settled in Police Station and just handed over the key to the affected person—police denied victims charges of being abused by caste name. Proper action not taken.
Interventions	1. On 13.12.2011 victim directly reported to the office of Evidence. 2. Supportive counselling was given to him. 3. On the same day complaint was prepared on behalf of the victim. 4. On 14.12.2011 complaint was sent to the Human Rights Commission, Govt. authorities and police officials for appropriate action. 5. Except police enquiry no legal action taken against the caste Hindu instead the police find fault on the victim and tried to close the case as false given.
Impact	• Response received from National Commission for Scheduled Caste Chennai dated 21.12.2011. • Response received from SHRC Chennai dated 04.01.2012. • Response from National Commission for Scheduled Caste Chennai with report of Superintendent of Police, Thirunelveli dated 25.01.2012. • Strategically we were able to expose in getting justice to the affected by sending various complaints to various government mechanisms and Commissions. • Authentic documents were gathered by the

	team to prosecute the perpetrators. • Due to our assistance the Dalit victim able to approach the legal system to seek redress. • The Dalit victim is now well aware of the laws to reclaim their rights related to land. • Reply received from SP Thirunelveli dated 18.01.2012. • On the intervention of Evidence, the house was retrieved and got back his ownership.
List of Documents	1. Certificate of person with disabilities to the victim. 2. House site patta issued to the victim dated 22.02.2000. 3. House tax receipt. 4. Copy of complaint by the victim dated 13.12.2011. 5. Response received from National Commission for Scheduled Caste Chennai dated 21.12.2011. 6. Response received from SHRC Chennai dated 04.01.2012. 7. Reply received from SP Thirunelveli dated 18.01.2012.

Source: Evidence Documents.

20. Dalit Kumar was abused in caste name and attempted to murder his brother by the caste Hindu over a purchase of a house at Krishnaberi Village, Sivakasi Taluk, Virudhunagar District

Name of the Affected	Kumar (30)
Religion/Caste/Sex	Hindu/Parayar/Male
Address	1/51, Ambedkar Colony, Kriashnaberi Village T. Managacheri Post Malli (Via) Sivakasi Taluk Virudhunagar District
Incident in Brief	Dalit Kumar and his brother Maran (28) S/o Senkolraj a resident of Krishnaperi Village at Virudhunagar district was abused in caste name, brutally assaulted and attempted to murder by caste Hindu Yoga Ganesh and his associate over a purchase of house from a Dalit without the knowledge of the caste Hindu and refused to

	vacate the house.
Name of the accused/caste	1. Mr. Yoga Ganesh (28)/Maravar 2. Mr. Pulugandi (25)/Maravar 3. Mr. Sudarsanan (19)/Maravar 4. Mr. Karuppasami (55)/Maravar 5. Mr. Arumugham (40)/Maravar 6. Ms. Muneswari (23)/Maravar
Struggles/Obstacles faced by the victim	• The victim bought a house from a same community person which was occupied by the caste Hindu threatened the victim that how dare he can purchase when he had occupied the house. • The victim presented complaint courageously in the police against the caste Hindu atrocity.
Case registered details	Malli police registered FIR Cr.No. 3/2012 under sections 294(b), 307 I.P.C and 3(1) (x) and 3(2)(v) SC/ST Act, 1989 on 20.01.2012.
Interventions	1. On 3.01.2012 fact-finding was done by Evidence team 2. On 4.01.2012 victim reported to Evidence office directly. 3. Supportive counselling was given to the victim and his family members 4. Complaints preferred to State Human Rights Commission, National SC/ST Commission, Chief Secretary, DGP, ADW SC, District Collector Virudhunagar, SP Virudhunagar, DSP Srivilliputhur on 4.01.2012. 5. Petition under RTI Act was sent to know the present stage of case on 23.02.2012.
Impact	• Malli police had registered FIR in Cr.No. 3/2012 under IPC section 294(b), 307 r/w 3(1) (5), 3(1)(10), 3(2) (5), 3(1) (10), 3(2) (5) SC/ST Act. • Strategically we were able to expose in getting justice to the affected by sending various complaints to various government mechanisms and Commissions. • Authentic documents were gathered by the team to prosecute the perpetrators. • Response received from National Commission for Scheduled Caste, Chennai on 13.01.2012. • Reply under RTI Act dated 29.03.2012. • It is known that charge sheet was sent to the Court by the police.
List of Documents	1. Proceedings of the land acquirement dated

	16.09.2001. 2. Sale deed dated 21.12.2011. 3. Copy of FIR in Cr.No. 3/2012 dated 02.01.2012. 4. MLC issued dated 02.01.2012. 5. Copy of complaint by the victim dated 04.01.2012. 6. Response from National Commission for SC dated 13.01.2012.

Source: Evidence Documents.

21. Tribal woman Chandra's cultivated crops in her own land were destroyed by the caste Hindu Forest Officials in Kumbarayur Village, Kodaikanal Taluk, Dindigul District

Name of the Affected	Chandra (40)
Religion/Caste/Sex	Hindu/Parayar/Female
Address	W/o. Chandrasekaran 2/3/49 Adivasi Colony, Kumbarayur Village, Kumbarayur Post, Kodaikanal Taluk Dindigul District
Incident in Brief	Tribal woman Chandra's family have the benefit of the land and their cultivation plants were destroyed by the forest department without their knowledge when objected the affected were intimidated and abused in caste name by the caste Hindu Forest Officials in Kumpariyur village, Kodaikanal Taluk, Dindigul District.
Name of the accused/caste	1. Mr. Muthusami (56)/Thevar 2. Mr. Sakthivel (52)
Struggles/Obstacles faced by the victim	• Several years the victim had been sending petition to the concerned officials but no proper response. The government hassled by not giving patta without any reason. • Meanwhile, the victim faced annoyance from the Forest Officials
Case registered details	Nil
Interventions	1. On 07.11.2011 victim directly reported to the office. 2. Supportive counselling was given to him. 3. On the same day complaint was prepared on behalf of the victim. 4. On 18.11.2011 complaint was sent to the

	Human Rights Commission, Govt. Authorities and Police officials for appropriate action 5. On 12.05.2012, petition sent to the Deputy Tahsildar, Kodaikanal Taluk, Dindigul requesting patta.
Impact	• On 15.11.2011 reply letter received from National SC/ST Commission. • On 21.01.2011 reply letter received from SHRC. • On 25.11.2011 reply letter under RTI Act was received. • Strategically we were able to expose in getting justice to the affected by sending various government mechanisms and Commissions. • Authentic documents were gathered by the team to prosecute the perpetrators. • Due to our assistance the Dalit woman victim able to approach the legal system to seek redress. • The Dalit woman victim is now well aware of the laws to reclaim their rights related to land.
List of Documents	1. Petition sent to the District Collector to issue patta dated 22.08.2011. 2. Copy of complaint by the victim dated 08.11.2011. 3. Postal receipt. 4. Response from the National Commission for Scheduled Caste/Scheduled Tribe, Chennai dated 15.11.2011. 5. Response from State Human Rights Commission, Chennai dated 21.11.2011. 6. Response received from Public Information Officer cum P.A to District Collector, Dindigul dated 25.11.2011.

Source: Evidence Documents.

22. Dalit woman Palaniammal and 28 Dalits were struggling for 18 years entitled to get free house site patta for the government allotted group houses (Thokkuppu house) in Errampatti Village, Vadipatti Taluk, Madurai District

Name of the Affected	Palaniammal (48)
Religion/Caste/Sex	Hindu/Parayar/Female
Address	W/o. Selvam 1/32, M.G.R. Nagar, Errampatti Village,

	Errampatti Post, Alanganallur (via) Vadipatti Taluk Madurai District
Incident in Brief	Dalit Palaniyammal and 28 Dalit families were allotted house in the construction of group houses (Thokkuppu Veedu) by the government in 1994 but not provided house patta till now at Errampatti Village, Vadipatti Taluk, Madurai District.
Name of the accused/caste	Slackness of Revenue Officials
Struggles/Obstacles faced by the victim	• Dalit victim and 28 Dalit family members struggling for the past 18 years to get the house site patta allotted for them in the Thokuppu Veedu (group house).
Case registered details	Nil
Interventions	1. On 24.03.2012 victim Palaniammal directly reported to the office, supportive counselling was given to the victim 2. On the same day complaint was prepared based on the statement given by the victim. 3. On 24.03.2012 complaint was sent to the Revenue Officers and the District Collector, Madurai for issue of Patta.
Impact	• Strategically we were able to expose in getting justice to the affected by sending various government mechanisms and Commissions. • Authentic documents were gathered by the team to prosecute the perpetrators. • Due to our assistance the Dalit women able to approach the legal system to seek redress. • The Dalit woman victim is now well aware of the laws to reclaim their rights related to land.
List of Documents	1. Hcuse tax receipts. 2. Copy of complaint by the victim dated 02.03.2012. 3. Postal receipt.

Sources: Evidence Documents.

23. Dalit Velraj was abused in caste name and intimidated by the caste Hindu when objected for unauthorized occupant of his house in A. Vadipatti Village, Periakulam Taluk, Theni District

Name of the Affected	Velraj (29)
Religion/Caste/Sex	Hindu/Parayar/Male
Address	252 B-3, North Street, A. Vadipatti Village A. Vadipatti Post Periyakulam Taluk, Theni district
Incident in Brief	Dalit Velraj (29) S/o Nagaraj a resident of A. Vadipatti village at Theni district was abused in caste name and threatened to murder by caste Hindu Vetrivel, when the victim questioned about the unauthorized occupant of his house by the caste Hindu
Name of the accused/caste	Mr. Vetrivel (55) Chettiar Community
Struggles/Obstacles faced by the victim	• Dalit victim continuously fought for unauthorized occupant of house site by the caste Hindu. • In the year 2011 he preferred complaint to various officials and no proper action taken. • The police closed the case as civil dispute
Case registered details	Dalit victim preferred complaint and Jayamangalam police issued receipt No. 386/2011 dated 24.11.2011.
Interventions	1. On 04.02.2012 victim directly approached Evidence office. 2. Supportive counselling was given to the victim and his family members. 3. Complaints preferred to State Human Rights Commission, National SC/ST Commission, Chief Secretary, DGP, ADW SC District Collector Theni, DSP Periyakulam on 06.02.2012. 4. Petition under RTI Act was sent to know the present stage of the case on 09.03.2012. 5. Case was filed before High Court, Madurai Bench on 24.04.2012.
Impact	• National Commission for Scheduled Caste, Chennai sent with report of Superintendent of Police, Theni District on 13.01.2012.

	• Response received from National Commission for Scheduled Caste, Chennai on 27.02.2012. • Response from SHRC dated 14.03.2012. • Reply received under RTI Act dated 06.04.2012.
List of Documents	1. Copy of Maduri District Gazette for acquisition of Dalit land dated 14.07.1981. 2. House site patta. 3. Sale deed dated 04.10.2010. 4. House tax receipt dated 29.09.2011. 5. Encumbrance certificate dated 30.09.2011. 6. Receipt issued by Jayamangalam police in R. No. 386/11 dated 24.11.2011. 7. Copy of complaint by the victim dated 06.02.2012. 8. Response from National Commission for SC Chennai dated 05.03.2012 with report of Superintendent of Police, Theni. 9. Response from SHRC Chennai dated 14.03.2012.

Source: Evidence Documents.

24. Dalit woman Selvakani's land was transferred with forged document by the caste Hindu when objected she was intimidated and humiliated in V. Adichanallur Village, Srivaikuntam Taluk, Thoothukudi District

Name of the Affected	Selvakani (45)
Religion/Caste/Sex	Hindu/Parayar/Female
Address	W/o. Subramanian 2/109, Subramaniapuram South Street V. Adichanallur Village, V. Adichanallur Post Srivaikuntam Taluk, Thoothukudi District
Incident in Brief	Dalit women Selvakani and her husband were humiliated and threatened to murder by caste Hindu Nallakannu since victim objected the caste Hindu for transferring her land in the name of a caste Hindu with forged document in Athichanallur Village, Srivaikuntam Taluk at Thoothukudi District
Name of the accused/caste	1. Mr. Nallakannu (45) Maravar
Struggles/Obstacles faced by the victim	• Dalit victim fought against the unscrupulous caste Hindu who transferred her land with forged document.

	• The matter was known to her when the victim applied for encumbrance certificate. • Till now the victim and her family members are facing threat and abused in caste name by the caste Hindus. • The victim could not seek loan from the bank to cultivate crops in her own land due to the recent land dispute. Victim's livelihood rights were denied to atrocity.
Case registered details	Dalit victim preferred complaint before Superintendent of Police (land grab cell) Thoothukudi district on 10.01.2012. On 22.04.2012 victim preferred police complaint against Nallakannu and his associate in Srivaikuntam station stating that the accused are threatening and attempt to assault due to the previous motive over land dispute. The Crime No. 86/12 u/s 427, 506(ii) IPC.
Interventions	1. On 4.2.2012 victim directly approached Evidence office. 2. Supportive counselling was given to the victim and family members. 3. Complaints preferred to State Human Rights Commission, National SC/ST Commission, Chief Secretary, DGP, ADW SC, District Collector Thoothukudi, SP Thoothukudi, DSP Thiruvaigundam, RDO Thoothukudi on 06.02.2010.
Impact	• On 14.02.2012 National Commission for Scheduled Castes, Chennai forwarded a letter to Additional Director General of Police, Chennai to take necessary action. • Response received from SHRC Chennai dated 14.03.2012. • Strategically we were able to expose in getting justice to the affected by sending various complaints to various government mechanism and Commissions. • Authentic documents were gathered by the team to prosecute the perpetrators. • Due to our assistance the Dalit women able to approach the legal system to seek redress. • The Dalit woman victim is now well aware of the laws to reclaim their rights related to land.
List of Documents	1. Patta issued to the victim 2. Chitta 3. Adangal document 4. Land tax receipt 5. Forged document prepared as power of attorney by caste Hindu Nallakannu Gounder dated 21.09.1992

	6. Sale deed by Madasami to the victim dated 12.06.1996. 7. Sale deed dated 18.08.2011 8. Encumbrance certificate dated 8.12.2011 9. Copy of complaint by the victim dated 06.02.2012 10. Response from National Commission for SC Chennai dated 14.02.2012

Sources: Evidence Documents.

25. Dalit woman Chinnaponnu was cheated producing false documents by the caste Hindus when she was abused in caste name and assaulted in Kollampalayam Village, Thiruchengodu Taluk in Namakkal District

Name of the Affected	Chinnaponnu (37)
Religion/Caste/Sex	Hindu/Arunthathiar/Female
Address	W/o.Kumar Arunthathiar Street Kollampalayam Village Kolikkal Natham Post Thiruchengodu Taluk Namakkal District
Incident in Brief	Dalit woman Chinnaponnu (37) W/o Kumar a resident of Kallapalayam village, Thiruchenkodu Taluk, Namakkal district was abused in caste name and assaulted by caste Hindu Shanmugasundaram due to land dispute
Name of the accused/caste	1. Mr. Shanmugasundaram (47) Mudaliar 2. Mr. Veluchami (45) Mudaliar 3. Ms. Nalini (29) Mudaliar 4. Mr. Pandian
Struggles/Obstacles faced by the victim	• The victim gave complaint for cheating against the caste Hindu. • The victim was abused in caste name and threatened and humiliated when she fought against the caste Hindus.
Case registered details	District Crime Branch PS Cr.No. 13/2011 under sections 420, 506(i), 468, 465 I.P.C. dated 04.07.2011.
Interventions	1. On 07.07.2011 Evidence Fact Finding team collected the true facts. 2. On 08.07.2011, Press release was issued to

	sensitize the issue to the public. 3. On 17.07.2011 victim directly reported to the office and supportive counselling was given to the victim 4. On 22.07.2011 complaint preferred to State Human Rights Commission, National SC/ST Commission, State Women Commission, Chief Secretary, DGP, ADW SC, District Collector Namakkal, SP Namakkal and DSP Namakkal. 5. On 14.11.2011 petition under RTI was sent to SP Namakkal to know the present status of case.
Impact	• On 04.07.2011 District Crime Branch Namakkal had registered FIR in Cr.No. 13/2011 u/s 420 506(i), 468, 465, IPC. • Accused was arrested by the police. • Due to our timely intervention the accused came forward to repay the amount of Rs. 2 lakhs and 20,000 was repaid for the land and settled the dispute amicably. • Strategically we were able to expose in getting justice to the affected by sending various complaints to various government mechanisms and Commissions. • Authentic documents were gathered by the team to prosecute the perpetrators. • Due to our assistance the Dalit woman was able to approach the legal system to seek redress. • The woman victim is now well aware of the laws to reclaim their rights related to land.
List of Documents	1. Encumbrance certificate dated 11.07.2011. 2. Patta issued to the victim. 3. Forgery sale deed by the caste Hindu Veluchami and Nalini dated 23.10.2009. 4. Copy of FIR in Cr.No. 13/2011 dated 04.07.2011. 5. Press release dated 08.07.2011. 6. Copy of complaint by the victim dated 18.07.2011.

Source: Evidence Documents.

26. Tribal Pulayar Chinnaiah was threatened to kill when denied to sell his land to the caste Hindu at Poolatur Village, Kodaikanal Taluk, Dindigul District

Name of the Affected	Chinnaiah (36).
Religion/Caste/Sex	Tribal/Parayar/Male
Address	J.P. Nagar

	Poolathur Village Poolathur Post Kodaikanal Taluk Dindigul District
Incident in Brief	Tribal Chinnaiya (36) S/o Vembuliyan @ Mayandi a resident of Poolathur village at Dindigul district was abused and threatened to murder by a caste Hindu because victim denied selling his land to the caste Hindu.
Name of the accused/caste	Mr. Agamudainambi (60)
Struggles/Obstacles faced by the victim	• The Dalit victim fought against the neighbouring caste Hindu landowners. • The victim preferred complaint to the police with courage to get justice.
Case registered details	Nil
Interventions	1. On 26.12.2011 victim Chinnaiya directly reported to the office. 2. Supportive counselling was given to the victim 3. On the same day complaint was prepared on behalf of the victim. 4. On 27.12.2011 complaint was sent to the Human Rights Commisssion, Govt. authorities and police officials for appropriate action. 5. On 20.02.2012, petition under RTI Act was sent to know the stage of the case.
Impact	• On 02.01.2012 reply letter received from National SC/ST Commission. • On 13.01.2012 reply received from SHRC Chennai. • Strategically we were able to expose in getting justice to the affected by sending various complaints to various government mechanisms and Commissions. • Authentic documents were gathered by the team to prosecute the perpetrators. • Due to our assistance the victim was able to approach the legal system to seek redress. • The victim is now well aware of the laws to reclaim their rights related to land.
List of Documents	1. Sale deed dated 28.07.1998 2. Agreement for sale of land dated 14.06.2011 3. Encumbrance certificate dated 19.08.2011. 4. Copy of complaint by the victim dated 27.12.2011. 5. Response from National Commission for SC

	dated 02.01.2012. 6. Response from SHRC dated 13.01.2012.

Sources: Evidence Documents.

27. Tribal Irular woman Indira was abused in caste name and brutally assaulted when she objected to the illegal encroachment of her land by dominant caste of Kattachimedu village, Chenji Taluk in Viluppuram District

Name of the Affected	Indira (40)
Religion/Caste/Sex	Hindu/Tribal Irular/Female
Address	W/o. Patchamuthu Murugan Kovil Street, Kattachimedu Village, Melasevur Post Chenji Taluk Viluppuram District
Incident in Brief	Tribal Irular woman Indir's (40) W/o Pitchaimuthu land was encroached by caste Hindu Jayaraman and his family members. While she intervened and questioned about it she and her husband were abused by the caste Hindu in Kattachimedu Village, Chenji Taluk, Viluppuram District.
Name of the accused/caste	1. Mr. Jayaraman (35)/Gounder 2. Ms. Amutha (30)/Gounder 3. Mr. Kuppan (55)/Gounder
Struggles/Obstacles faced by the victim	• Since one year the caste Hindus were creating nuisance to the victim and her family members who are the only Tribal living in the midst of caste Hindus. • The whole family was undergoing mental suffering and living in a dreadful situation. • The victim and her family members were tortured frequently by the caste Hindu with intention to grab the land illegally. • But the victim continuously fought against their annoyance.
Case registered details	Chenji Police Station Cr.No. 368/1010 under Sections 294, 323 I.P.C r/w 3(1)(x) SC/ST Act, 1989 on 27.07.2010
Interventions	1. Fact-finding was done by Evidence team on 10.06.2011. 2. Educated the woman victim to understand

	the laws relating to land rights violations and stop getting exploited by their opponents. 3. Complaint preferred to State Human Rights Commission, National SC/ST Commission, State Women Commission, Chief Secretary, DGP, ADW SC, District Collector, Villupuram, Superintendent of Police of Vilupuram, DSP, Chenji on 27.06.2011. 4. Petition under RTI Act was sent to know the stage of the case on 01.08.2011.
Impact	• Chenji. Police had registered FIR in Cr.No. 368/10 under IPC section 294, 323, r/w3(1)(10) SC/ST Act. • Authentic documents were gathered by the team to prosecute the perpetrators. • Due to our assistance, Trible woman was able to approach the legal system to seek redress. • The woman victim is now well aware of the laws to reclaim their rights related to land. • PRC No. 19/2010 was pending with Judicial Magistrate, Chenji. • The National Commission for Scheduled Caste, Chennai forwarded the copy of complaint to the Tribal Welfare Department, Chennai for taking proper action on 01.07.2011. • A sum of Rs. 6250 was given compensation to the victim on 03.08.2011.
List of Documents	15. Land tax receipts. 16. Copy of FIR in Cr.No. 368/2010 dated 27.07.2010. 17. Copy of complaint of the victim dated 24.06.2011. 18. Letter of National Commission for Scheduled Caste, Chennai dated 01.07.2011. 19. Copy of cheque for Rs. 6250 dated 03.08.2011.

Source: Evidence Documents.

28. Dalit woman Alagumeena and her son were abused in caste name and brutally assaulted by caste Hindu over the issue on illegal sand mining in their own land in Vembarpatti Village, Dindigul Taluk and District

Name of the Affected	Alagumeena (51)
Religion/Caste/Sex	Hindu/Pallan/Female
Address	369/2 Santhanamariyamman Koil Street Vembarpatti Village Vembarpatti Post, Dindigul Taluk Dindigul District
Incident in Brief	Dalit woman Alagumeena (51) S/o Marimuthu and her son Alagesan a resident of Vembarpatti Village, Dindigul District was abused in caste name and brutally assaulted by the caste Hindu Logu and his brother when they intervened and questioned about illegal sand mining from their land.
Name of the accused/caste	1. Mr. Logu @ Prabakaran (30)/Reddiyar 2. Mr. Kannan (48)/Reddiyar
Struggles/Obstacles faced by the victim	• Even after submitting of several complaints there was no proper action taken by the police against the caste Hindus. • Police forced the Dalits to go for a compromise and were favouring the caste Hindus. • Though it is a MLC case no FIR registered against the accused till now.
Case registered details	On 08.04.2011, complaint was given at Shanarpatti Police Station Dindigul District and pending.
Interventions	1. On 21.07.2011 victim directly reported to the office. 2. Supportive counselling was given to the victim. 3. Complaint preferred to State Human Rights Commission, National SC/ST Commission, State Women Commission, Chief Secretary, DGP, ADW SC, District Collector Dindigul, SP Dindigul, DSP Dindigul on 21.07.2011 4. On 07.09.2011 Follow-up Petition sent to National SC/ST Commission. 5. On 15.11.2011 Petition under RTI Act was sent to SP Dindigul to know the present status of the case.
Impact	• Response received from State Human Rights Commission on 02.08.2011. • Response received from National SC/ST Commission on 17.08.2011. • Reply under RTI Act was received on 29.11.2011. • Strategically we were able to expose in getting justice to the affected by sending

	various complaints to various government mechanism and Commissions. • Authentic documents were gathered by the team to prosecute the perpetrators. • Due to our assistance Dalit woman was able to approach the legal system to seek redress. • The woman victim is now well aware of the laws to reclaim their rights related to the land.
List of Documents	1. Agreement document to victim's daughter Karpukarasi dated 13.12.2010. 2. Land tax receipt. 3. Copy of complaint by the victim to the Shanarpatti police dated 14.07.2011. 4. Medical summary certificate for Alagesan dated 18.07.2011. 5. Copy of complaint by the victim dated 21.07.2011. 6. Response from State Human Rights Commission, Chennai dated 02.08.2011. 7. Response from National Commission for Scheduled Caste, Chennai dated 17.08.2011. 8. Reply under RTI Act dated 29.11.2011.

Source: Evidence Documents.

29. Dalit Anand @ Asuranath and his community member's cultivated crops were destroyed by the Forest Rangers when objected the forest official and the police filed false cases against the victims at Chotthuparai, Periakulam Taluk, Theni District

Name of the Affected	Anand @ Asuranath (29)
Religion/Caste/Sex	Hindu/Parayar/Male
Address	S/o Dhanushkodi (Late) 4/6/12A, Nayagam Street, T. Kallipatti Village, T. Kallipatti Post Periyakulam Taluk, Theni District
Incident in Brief	Dalit Asuranath and 45 Dalit community families people have benefitted the land which belong to revenue department for many years. But without any notification the forest officials destroyed all the cultivated crops in the land domicile by the Dalits. The affected Dalits protested against the forest officials action. So the police officials filed false complaint against them in T. Kallupatti village, Periyakulam Taluk, Theni District.

Name of the accused/caste	1. Mr. Lakshmanan, Forest Official 2. Mr. Boopathy 3. Mr. Selvakumar
Struggles/Obstacles faced by the victim	• The victim and community people staged demonstration against the forest officials as they destroyed benefited land crops. • At the same time, the Dalit victims prayed to issue patta several times. • The Dalit victims faced with brave heart against the false cases filed by the police officers.
Case registered details	Dalit victim presented complaint and the police issued receipt no. 425/09 dated 27.11.2009.
Interventions	1. On 13.12.2011 victim directly reported to the office. 2. Supportive counselling was given to the victims. 3. On the same day complaint was prepared on behalf of the victim 4. On 14.12.2011 complaint was sent to the Human Rights Commission, Govt authorities and police officials for appropriate action. 5. On 17.02.2012, petition under RTI Act was sent to know the stage of the case.
Impact	• On 27.12.2011, response received from National Commission for Scheduled Caste, Chennai • Response received from State Human Rights Commission, Chennai dated 05.01.2012. • Strategically we were able to expose in getting justice to the affected by sending various complaints to various government mechanism and Commission. • Authentic documents were gathered.
List of Documents	1. House tax receipts. 2. Copy of complaint by the victim dated 09.08.2011.

Source: Evidence Documents.

Section III

Observation

Many advocates lamented about the poor rate of conviction of cases registered on the atrocities committed on the Dalits. While seeing the presentation of cases before a panel of juries one could easily notice the loopholes in the cases of Dalits filed by the advocates. Though steps were taken to give lands to the Dalits through schemes of the Government the Dalits could not keep the lands with them. Their object conditions made them to borrow money which ultimately deprived them of their lands. Further, the caste Hindus lured the Dalits by making several designs. Though the Dalits consider land as a source of income and a source of pride and identity, they could not retain with them as other caste groups did. In every village they are isolated and are kept with low esteem. Their powerlessness enabled the dominant caste groups to exploit the Dalits easily. This is a general scenario.

Secondly, the Dalits do not have support structure at the ground level as Dalits face volley of problems at the community level. There are organisations and groups doing policy advocacy for Dalits at a higher level. There are very many institutions undertaking research on the issues of Dalits but very few organisations and institutions are working with affected people at the community level. But there is no worthwhile organisation to support the Dalits when they face problems in the community. After the establishment of the New Panchayati Raj System in India after the enactment of the 73rd Amendment to the Constitution of India, more number of Dalit representatives is included for governance and thereby the struggle is intensified at the grass roots for social justice.

Thirdly, the Dalits do not have needed awareness on their rights. They are continuously mobilised for political activities as vote banks but they are not mobilized for development. They lack neither political awareness nor development awareness. Despite the presence of strong media, political outfits for Dalits, higher learning institutions level of awareness among the Dalits on development is low.

Fourthly, when organisations are taking up the cases of the Dalits, they file cases on the atrocities committed against Dalits under PCR Act. But cases have not been framed strongly with adequate evidences. Further, while framing charges, the legal authorities have invoked one part of the PCR Act which is meant for discriminative practices not for retrieving the lands. There is yet another part in the same Act which deals with the protection of land rights. Absolutely while framing cases that part is not taken into account and as a result the Dalits are losing their lands.

Fifthly, the Panchayats have a mandatory role to administer social justice. But nobody is there to supervise the Panchayats whether they perform the mandatory function of administering social justice. On all the cases Panchayats could have played a vital role but they have not played such role. At a higher level an officer can look after the functions of Gram Panchayat in administrating social justice. One state level official can monitor the social justice function of the Panchayats.

Sixthly, one should not seek justice in the Court. It is a costly venture for Dalits. The Dalits have to organsie themselves and they have to agitate against all kind of atrocities committed against them. Of the twenty nine cases, a few have won in their struggle because they fought against injustice done to them. Dalits have to be mobilized and they are to be organsied. Equally they are to be trained to struggle against injustice. They should also be sensitized finally a private member bill can be moved in State Legislative Assembly to protect the Dalits land rights and thereby the Government can be sensitised.

Conclusion

The very birth of Dalit political outfits has questioned the claim of the advocates of Dravidian movement that it works for the upliftment of the poorest of the poor non-Brahmin in Tamil Nadu. It is Periyar land and in the Periyar movement Dalits have integrated themselves with the hope that their conditions will be changed and ameliorated. For the past forty years Dravidian political parties both the DMK and the AIADMK have been in power alternatively. Yet the social justice is problematic in this province despite proliferation of welfare schemes and populist schemes. For the past forty years, the Most Backward Class and Dalits have moved away from the Dravidian Movement and they formed their own political outfits by arguing that the major benefits of governance under the DMK and the AIADMK have benefited the backward classes alone and not the poor.

Subsequently, the 73rd Amendment to the Constitution of India has put a test to the Dravidian movement. After the first general election to the new rural local bodies in 1996, reality of the conditions of the Dalits in the rural areas came to the surface.

When Dalits came to power in rural local bodies, Dalits expect much from the Dalit representatives. Later it is realized that neither the Dalit representatives nor the Dalits are empowered through this new process of decentralization of powers. One could see the conflict syndrome in many of the rural local bodies. Against this background series of studies have been conducted by "Evidence" an organization working with Dalits for Dalit empowerment. The studies have been conducted not for knowledge sake. They are meant for action and policy advocacy. Evidence emerged as support structure for the Dalit victims. All the studies have been scientifically designed and professionally carried out. From the studies conducted in rural Tamil Nadu a few points emerged clearly. The discriminatory practices both in form and intensity have not been reduced as expected because of the Dravidian movement. Intensity and forms of discriminations vary from place to place. Equally, the elected Dalit representatives also face such a kind of discriminations. They are being controlled by a careful design of the caste Hindus and other dominant groups. In the village Panchayats vice-Presidents and clerks are the non-Dalits. Vice-presidents and the Panchayat clerks belonging to caste Hindus and other dominant groups have established their supremacy over Dalit Panchayat Presidents. Hence, the Dalit Panchayat leaders are not able to function independently. The Dalit Panchayat leaders repeatedly requesting the Government to reserve the post of Vice-presidents to Dalits as the post of Presidents. When the President post is reserved for Dalits, along with, the vice-President's post is also to be reserved for Dalits. This has been the plea of the Dalit representatives for long. Dalit representatives are not properly and professionally trained for governance and administration. They demanded a special training for them and it has to be designed exclusively for Dalits. There is yet another demand that the training for Dalit representatives should be given not by Government training institutions but it should be given by organsations which are working with Dalits for Dalit empowerment.

Dalit representatives are not allowed to take up the social justice issues in the meeting of Gram Sabha and the Panchayats. Further major segment of the Dalit representatives are drawn towards the Panchayat by other groups. They themselves admitted that well qualified candidates from the Dalit community have contested in the election. But they were all defeated. They further admitted that they are all poor and yet spent money for elections. But somebody has spent money for them. It is also inferred from the above responses that the economic profile of the elected Dalit representatives was very weak. Moreover, the Dalit representatives are lured to the design of the caste Hindus or other dominant groups knowingly or unknowingly. So, the majority Panchayats which are headed by Dalit representatives are indirectly controlled by the dominant caste groups. When Dalit representatives are echoing their grievances, the Dalit political parties are not taking up the causes of the Dalit Panchayat presidents. Dalit political parties can closely work with the Panchayati Raj System as Panchayat has got tremendous potential to deliver goods for the Dalits. Generally, Dalits are not aware of their rights. There is no development mobilization of Dalits. Dalit Panchayat leaders can take up Dalit component plan in Panchayat by evolving a micro plan for the Panchayats. Dalits are not aware that their lands can be reclamated by using the Mahatma Gandhi National Employment Guarantee Scheme. They are not aware of it. When Dalit land rights issues are taken to the judiciary cases have not been filed with adequate evidences and safeguards. Hence, on many occasions Dalits have to lose their case. Dalit Panchayat leaders do not have any association or federation as other leaders to focus their problems. The Dalit Panchayat leaders do not get adequate support from the lower level bureaucracy and equally they are humiliated in the offices by the lower level officials. Their ignorance is being exploited by all. To come out from all the problems they need information, empowerment, organisation and support structure. Organisations which are working with the Dalits on their causes should guide them properly and build their capacity to manage the problems. There are remarkable success stories from the Dalits. We have to analyse the success stories and we have to guide on the factors which are basic for the empowerment and emancipation of Dalits.

Notes

1. C.J. Fuller, *Caste Today,* New Delhi: Oxford University Press, 1997, pp. 1-31.
2. Gail Omvedt, *Dalits and the Democratic Revolution,* New Delhi: Sage Publications, 1994.
3. Pratap Bhanu Mehta, "Affirmation and Reservation", *Economic and Political Weekly,* Vol. XXIV, No. 7, 2006.
4. Baldev Raj Nayar, *The Myth of the Shrinking State: Globalization and the State in India,* New Delhi: Oxford University Press, 2009
5. Gerald E. Caiden, "The Repositioning of Public Governance: Global Experience and Challenges" in Bidyut Charkrabarty and Mohit Bhattacharya (eds.), *The Governance Discourse: A Reader,* New Delhi: Oxford University Press, 2008, pp. 103-131.
6. Gopal Guru, "Social Justice" in Niraja Gopal Jayal and Pratap Bhanu Mehta (eds.), *The Oxford Companion to Politics in India,* New Delhi: Oxford University Press, 2010, pp. 365-380.
7. K.C. Sivaramakrishnan, *Power to the People,* New Delhi: Konark Publishers Pvt. Ltd., 2000.
8. S.C. Dube, *Indian Society,* New Delhi: National Book Trust, 1992.
9. Neera Desai and Usha Thakkar, *Women in Indian Society,* New Delhi: National Book Trust, 2001.
10. Kripa Ananthpur, *Rivalry or Synergy? Formal and Informal Local Governance in Rural India,* (Working Paper 226), Sussex: Institute of Development Studies, 2004.
11. T.S. Epstein, *South India: Yesterday, Today and Tomorrow,* New Delhi: Holmes and Meier Publications, Inc., 1973.
12. G. Palanithurai, *Rajiv Gandhi's Vision on Local Governance,* New Delhi: Concept Publishing Company (P) Ltd., 2001.
13. Aniruth Krishna, "Local Politics" in Niraja Gopal Jayal and Pratap Bhanu Mehta (eds.), *The Oxford Companion to Politics in India,* New Delhi: Oxford University Press, 2010, pp. 299-315.
14. G. Palanithurai, "Constitutional Laws *Vs* Community Laws in India: Conflict and Synergy", *The Grassroots Governance Journal,* Vol. V, No. 2, December, 2007.

15. J.S. Mill, *Utilitarianism: On Liberty and Consideration of Representative Government,* London: Tontana, 1976.
16. Myron Weiner, *The Indian Paradox: Essays in Indian Politics,* New Delhi: Sage Publications, pp. 21-22.
17. Hiranmay Karlekar (ed.), *Independent India: The First Fifty Years,* New Delhi: Oxford University Press, 1998, pp. 227-350.
18. G. Palanithurai, *A Framework for Devolution of Powers and Democracy and Development (monograph),* Gandhigram: Rajiv Gandhi Chair for Panchayati Raj Studies, 2004.
19. G. Palanithurai, "Status of Dalits and Dalit Gram Panchayat Leaders in Tamil Nadu" in Rakesh Hooja and Sunil Dutt (eds.), *Fifty Years of Panchayati Raj and Decentralized Development,* New Delhi: Indian Institute of Public Administration, 2009.
20. Indhu Rajagopal, *The Tyranny of Caste: The Non-Brahman Movement and Political Development in South India,* New Delhi: Vikas Publishing House, 1985, pp. 117-141.
21. T.G. Jacob and P. Bandhu, *Reflections on the Caste Question: The Dalit Situation in South India,* Ootacamsend, ODYSSEY, 2009.
22. G. Palanithurai, *Third General Election to Local Governments in Tamil Nadu: Expectations and Shocking Realities,* New Delhi: Concept Publishing Company (P) Ltd., 2007.
23. G. Palanithurai, *Remembering G.K. Moopanar,* New Delhi: Concept Publishing Company (P) Ltd.
24. P.S. Krishnan, Budget 2011-12 and the Scheduled Castes and Scheduled Tribes, *Frontline,* Vol. 28, No. 7, 2011.
25. Swati Bhattacharjee, Raghabendra Chattopadhyay, "The Information Deficit: Use of Media in a Deliberative Democracy", *Economic and Political Weekly,* Vol. XLVI, No. 52, December 2011, pp. 45-52.
26. G. Palanithurai and R. Ramesh, *Globalization and Rural Development*, New Delhi: Concept Publishing Company (P) Ltd., 2010.
27. G. Saravanan, "Women Panchayat President Victimized for being a Dalit", *The New Indian Express,* 15th March, 2009.
28. G. Palanithurai, *Performance of Dalits and Women Panchayat Leaders,* New Delhi: Concept Publishing Company (P) Ltd., 2006; S.N. Chaudhary, *Dalit and Tribal Leadership in Panchayats,* New Delhi: Concept Publishing Company (P) Ltd., 2004.
29. Jayshree Mansu Bhai, Aloysius Irudayam S.J. and Emma Sydenham, *Dalit Women's Right to Participation in Rural Panchayati Raj,* The Netherlands: Justitia et pax, 2009.
30. Express News Service, "Dalits allege threat to life, leave village en masse", *The New Indian Express,* 29th October, 2008.

31. Pratap Bhanu Mehta, *The Burden of Democracy*, New Delhi: Penguin Books, 2001, pp. 57-104.
32. P.S. Krishnan, Budget 2011-12 and the Scheduled Castes and Scheduled Tribes, *Frontline,* Vol. 28, No. 7, 2011.
33. G. Palanithurai, *Dalit Leadership in Panchayats (Monograph),* Gandhigram: Rajiv Gandhi Chair for Panchayati Raj Studies, 2003.
34. Yagati Chinna Rao (ed.), *Dividing Daltis: Writings on Sub-Categorization of Scheduled Caste,* New Delhi: Rawat Publications, 2009.
35. G. Palanithurai, G. Uma and M.A. Thirunavukkarasu, *Change Makers at Grassroots Democracy: Leadership Matters,* New Delhi: Concept Publishing Company (P) Ltd., 2007.
36. *The Hindu*, 22-07-2011.
37. *Frontline*, 8-4-2011, p. 4.
38. *Frontline*, 8-4-2011, Vol. 28, No. 7, April 2011.
39. D. Karthikeyan, "Electrified wall divides people on caste line: It serves to prevent Dalits from entering caste Hindu areas", *The Hindu,* 17th April, 2008.
40. S. Viswanathan, *"Dalits in Dravidian Land",* Chennai: Navayana, 2005.

Index

the education of the child had to ask themselves, Will this student, if admitted, succeed? The parents ask whether their child can do better on a particular course? The teachers also ask, "Will this child be able to copeup with the course"? The study bears the significance of answering such types of questions that arise before the admission of the students because a positive institutional climate will definitely bring out the best in the child. The study may be able to hand over new insight to concerned persons in taking decisions regarding institutional climate.

Schools play a critical role in the development of cognitive abilities, personality characteristics and values Institutions also serve as places that assist students in developing an understanding of society and commitment in political and civic engagement. In this regard also this study can be of immense help. When the cognitive abilities, personality characteristics and values are shaped accordingly, then the institutions can further help foster the knowledge, skills and dispositions that young people need to develop into politically aware and socially responsible individuals. This process is sometimes referred to as civic education. In today's political and educational climate civil learning will continue to remain on the margin unless it is incorporated into institutional accountability systems. This resource provides policy makers and practitioners with a vehicle for student and institution to meet out this need.

Institutional climate also include the school support for community based learning experiences. Sometimes teachers and students perceive symbolic and other non-observable elements of the school climate without being able to describe them clearly. In this direction also the study may be of great help. When the administrators and the components of the institutional climate will understand the role of institutional climate in development of cognitive abilities, per-